*D*edication and Acknowledgements

We have become friends with many people over the years through our travels. You may live far away, yet you are not far from our hearts. We have come to know other friends only through the mailbox--radio listeners, newsletter subscribers, and conference attendees. Thank you for bringing us joy and for telling us when we were mentioned in your prayers.

This book is dedicated to all of you, with thanksgiving.

Thanks also to Don Cooper of Servant Publications for publishing a number of my books and for being a good friend to us. (Lars has fond memories of their time together at the Frankfurt book fair in Germany, where Don was disturbed that my thrifty husband had brought a ninety-eight-cent can of smoked kippers from the States for his lunch, while he had to pay fifteen dollars for a mere hot dog, chips, and soda pop.)

Then there is Kathy Deering, who edited my newsletter for many years and who compiled the books taken from it. With gratitude, I also want to mention Linda Meyers, Kay Hill, Kathy Gilbert, Pat Cresoe, Jeannie Illges and Jan Wismer, who have all had a part in helping over the years.

—Elisabeth Elliot
Magnolia, Massachusetts

ELISABETH ELLIOT

BE STILL MY SOUL

SERVANT PUBLICATIONS
ANN ARBOR, MICHIGAN

Vine Books is an imprint of Servant Publications especially designed to
serve evangelical Christians.

Servant Mission Statement

We are dedicated to publishing books that spread the gospel of
Jesus Christ, help Christians to live in accordance with that
gospel, promote renewal in the church, and bear witness to
Christian unity.

Scripture verses marked NIV are from the *Holy Bible, New
International Version*. Verses marked KJV are from the *King James
Version*. Verses marked RSV are from the *Revised Standard Version* of
the Bible. Verses marked NASB are from the *New American Standard
Bible*. Verses marked PHILLIPS are from the *New Testament in Modern
English*, Revised Edition—J.B. Phillips, translator. Verses marked NEB
are from the *New English Bible*. Verses marked LB are taken from *The
Living Bible*.

Published by Servant Publications
P.O. Box 8617
Ann Arbor, Michigan 48107
www.servantpub.com

Cover design: Noah Pudgil

03 04 05 06 10 9 8 7 6 5 4 3 2 1

Printed in the United States of America
ISBN 1-56955-392-0

Library of Congress Cataloging-in-Publication Data

Elliot, Elisabeth.
  Be still my soul / Elisabeth Elliot.
      p. cm.
  ISBN 1-56955-392-0 (alk. paper)
  1. Christian life. 2. Christian women--Religious life. I. Title.
  BV4527.E44 2003
  248.4--dc22
                                        2003014601

Contents

Christ-Bearers

I have spent my life plumbing the depths of what it means to be a Christian. I am, as of this morning, still learning. One thing I learned a long time ago is that we have to receive the life of Christ ourselves before we can live it. We have to live it before we can give it to others. Receive, live, give. The theologians call this "incarnation," and it applies as much to us as Christians as it does to our Lord Himself.

Before Jesus was born, a young virgin named Mary responded to a heavenly summons and allowed God's Spirit to become flesh. She gave her body to be the chalice into which the life of God was poured. A chalice is a cup. What Mary did is what you and I are meant to do, every one of us, every day, no matter where we are or what the circumstances—to carry Christ into this world. We are like chalices, empty vessels willing and ready to be filled with the life of God. Cleaned out in the process, we are poured out for others. Our lives illustrate what God is like much more by what we *are* and *do* than by what we say. We incarnate Christ by taking up our crosses and following Him, doing exactly as Jesus did when He was obedient to the Father.

The word *incarnation* means "taking on flesh" or "being manifested in a human body." It comes directly from two words meaning "in the flesh" or "the enfleshing." God, who is Spirit, took on visible form for thirty-three years in the person of Jesus Christ. When Jesus died, the world could no longer see Him or touch Him. But because He gave us His Spirit when He rose from the dead and returned to His Father, Jesus made sure that the world could continue to see God in the flesh. The same Spirit that is in Him is in us Christians, "Christ in you, the hope of glory" (Colossians 1:27b). Even though Jesus may have become invisible to the eyes of people in the world, you and I are quite visible to them and to each other. In us, the world may in fact see God.

When the angel went to Mary, he said, "'Greetings, you who are highly favored! The Lord is with you.' Mary was greatly troubled at his words" (Luke 1:28-29, NIV). The angelic message was alarmingly clear and Mary's response was awe—and bewilderment. When something interrupts what we are doing (the angel interrupted Mary's housework, I suppose), most of us fret. God's message to Mary would have seemed to most engaged girls an enormous inconvenience, even a disaster. For her, it caused a moment of puzzlement (how could this be?). Then, as far as we know, she raised no objections about what would happen to her or her fiancé. Her answer came very simply, "Be it unto me according to Thy word."

Whether or not an angel ever comes to us, we might be troubled at some of God's words to us as well. We might wish we'd never heard them. But our response should be modeled on Mary's and that of her Son Jesus—immediate obedience. Like someone holding out a cup to be filled when a drink is offered, we need to put our hearts forward right when God offers to pour Himself into us for an assignment, large or small. It's the attitude of a Christ-bearer.

A writer once said, "Mary's was the purposeful emptiness of a virginal heart," not a formless emptiness without meaning. Like Mary, we are best suited as Christ-bearers if we too have a purposeful emptiness, a readiness to be filled. If we fill up on trivialities or anxieties, we won't have room in our hearts for Him.

For Christ-bearers, there is no dichotomy between secular work and spiritual work. There wasn't for Mary and there shouldn't be for us. Her work was to say yes to God's will and to follow through by doing the everyday tasks that needed to be done. She tended to the simple but time-consuming needs of her husband and family. She raised the baby Jesus into young manhood. She released Him to do the work of the kingdom of God.

Our life may seem more complicated than Mary's, but the basics are the same. We live in a continuum of visible, tangible things. We live with the washing machines that break down and the dinner that burns and bills to pay and traffic jams. It is an act of obedient surrender as you tend your small child with all his mess and endure sleepless nights and juggle your responsibilities at work and at home.

The baby Jesus would not only be fed at Mary's breast and learn at her feet and in the carpenter's shop, but He would one day feel the blindfold, the ropes, the lash, the thorns, and finally the blood, nails, and the splinters of the cross. The Lord of the universe had taken on the body of an ordinary, vulnerable, mortal man in order that He might suffer and be totally emptied and annihilated—to bring God's life into the world. "The bread which I will give is my own body and I shall give it for the life of the world" (John 6:51b, PHILLIPS). What bread do you and I have to give to the world?

We are meant to be chalices, life-bearers. As God's

expression of what He is like, we become broken bread and poured-out wine. There is no greater fullness.

❦ One ❦

Do We Know What We're In For?

One day as Jesus was walking beside the Sea of Galilee, He saw two fishermen, Simon Peter and his brother Andrew, casting a net into the lake. "Come, follow me," Jesus said, "and I will make you fishers of men" (Matthew 4:19). At once they left their nets and followed Him. Did they know what they were in for?

Jesus began at once to teach His new disciples. The sermon on the mountainside was His starting point, and it was a bombardment of seemingly impossible requirements. Then He proceeded to demonstrate His supernatural power to heal the sick and the blind, to calm a storm, to raise the dead. He reminded the disciples that the student should be like his teacher, the servant like his master—and that they would be able to do greater works than He did. They were warned not to be surprised if they should lose their lives for His sake. Jesus told them He must go to Jerusalem where He Himself would suffer many things, then die. This was too much for Peter. "Never, Lord!" he said. "This shall never happen to you!" For this, he received a stinging reply: "Get behind me, Satan! You are a stumbling block to me; you do not have in mind the things of God but the things of men" (Matthew 16:22-23). Then, immediately after speaking so scathingly, Jesus offered an invitation: "If anyone would [wants to, wills to, wishes to] come after me, he must deny himself and take up his cross and follow me" (Matthew 16:24).

The Cost Is High

Jesus never lured disciples by false advertising. Once, when great crowds were following Him, He turned to them and said, "If anyone comes to me and does not hate his father and mother, wife and children, brothers and sisters, even his own life, he cannot be a disciple of mine" (Luke 14:26, NEB). With terms like that, there was never a stampede to join Him when He walked the roads of Galilee. There is not likely to be one now.

He wanted followers, didn't He? Would Jesus ever make some kind of deal with potential recruits? Would He waive a few of the requisites? No. He added one more: "So also none of you can be a disciple of mine without parting with all his possessions" (Luke 14:33, NEB). Surely He exaggerates.

Does He? Twice He repeats His unequivocal words to great crowds. He is not speaking privately to the twelve whom He had instructed at length in the principles of discipleship, but to the masses. His message is: What I am asking is more than any of you can possibly give. You must ask for terms.

There is no hope for any of us until we confess our helplessness to be Christians. Then we are in a position to receive grace. There we have the "terms": grace—first, last, and always. So long as we see ourselves as competent we do not qualify. Jesus vividly depicted the obligations as beyond us. But "Come to me," He says. *Carry your cross and come with Me. I alone can make you a disciple.*

Like the twelve, we would-be disciples are "foolish and slow of heart to believe." We don't know what we're in for, but we're signed up and we're pretty sure we want to go all the way with Him. However, we are hampered by our preference for familiar comforts, and even sometimes by our exalted notions of the noble sacrifices we will make for the Cause. We miss the significance of the very sacrifices that count the most, the ones that convey our hearts to the One who has purchased us with His blood.

The first sacrifices in the Bible were those of Cain and Abel. Cain was a tiller of the soil and he offered grain, and Abel was a hunter who offered blood. God accepted Abel's sacrifice but rejected Cain's. Cain was infuriated, murderously so. But the problem was not in the choice of sacrificial substance, it was a matter of the heart. Cain's sacrifice was not offered from a trusting heart. "By faith, Abel offered God a better sacrifice than Cain did. By faith he was commended as a righteous man, when God spoke well of his offerings. And by faith he still speaks, even though he is dead" (Hebrews 11:4, NIV).

When a little boy comes to his mother with his sweaty fists full of smashed dandelions, there is nothing intrinsically valuable in the gift, but it is welcomed by her simply because her own son has offered it. When I was little I used to ask my father for money so I could buy him a present, and my father would give me a dime. In those days, a dime could buy a whole box of chocolates. So I would go to the drugstore and buy candy for my daddy. It wasn't chocolates that he wanted and he had given me the purchase price in the first place, but he was delighted with my small present.

No Turning Back
If we have chosen the narrow way, it is fortunate for us that we cannot always find a way to go back. We are committed—we have trusted God and agreed with His objective, though we do not know all that this is going to mean.

An early lesson in commitment is a ride on a roller coaster. Remember the eager waiting at the gate, the rush to climb in when the cars came clattering to a stop at the platform, the ecstasy with which you gripped the cold steel of the guardrail in front of you, the first steep climb over the top—only to see the tracks dropping away

beneath you? You gasped at what you were about to d
The impossibility of changing your mind was an awful
revelation. Why are so many of us willing to pay to have
ourselves helplessly flung through the air like this, sick-
eningly plunged and whirled and jerked? The worst of it,
the part that doesn't bother children, is that the train isn't
going anywhere. You've had this terrible ride just for the
ride?

The initial choice to go the whole way with God is
made, of necessity, in ignorance of all that will follow. We
have been warned that the road will be a hard one, for our
Master Himself walked a hard road, and He reminds us
that servants are not greater than their masters. But if,
given all the previews of what is coming, we have never-
theless set our faces to follow the Pioneer of Faith, there
will be many times along the road when we look over our
shoulder, longing, like the Israelites on the way to the
Promised Land, for the "leeks, the onions, and the garlic"
of our slavery (Numbers 11:5, RSV). We are fortunate,
then, that it is hard to find a way back.

During my first year in the jungle, before I married Jim,
I lost my informant as well as all my language materials.
It was as though God said to me, "What did you expect?
You gave everything to me when you were twelve years
old. When you were a young woman, you told me that you
would go anywhere that I wanted you to go. You prayed,

will in my life at any cost.' And so
...nt is killed and Jim's station is demol-
...d you lose your language materials, is
tha. ...ss? It's Mine. I can do what I want with
what you have given to Me."

The cost of discipleship seemed pretty steep.

🔥 The Joy Paradox

What is the result? Paradoxically (and generations of
Christians will back this up) it is *joy.* "Jesus,... for the joy
that was set before him endured the cross, despising the
shame, and is seated at the right hand of the throne of
God" (Hebrews 12:2, RSV). We don't have to wait for
heaven to have the joy; it comes to us regularly right here
on earth. The Lord Himself disciples us so that we can
share the joy of our Master. A merciful Father strips us as
a tree is stripped of its blossoms before it can bear fruit. He
is not finished with us yet, whatever the losses we suffer.
As we loose our hold on visible things, the invisible ones
become more precious. Where our treasure is, there will
our hearts be (Matthew 6:21).

Once an earnest young man asked what worldly things

he must forsake for the sake of Christ. The answer was very specific:

Colored clothes, for one thing. Get rid of everything in your wardrobe that is not white. Stop sleeping on a soft pillow. Sell your musical instruments and don't eat any more white bread. You cannot, if you are sincere about obeying Christ, take warm baths or shave your beard. To shave is to lie against Him who created us, to attempt to improve on His work.

Sound absurd? It was a sincere response and it was given in the most celebrated Christian schools of the second century A.D. We can all think of contemporary counterparts. Does "giving up worldly things" buy us a ticket to bliss?

There was nothing distinctively ascetic about Jesus. He ate what other people ate, drank what they drank—and even in questionable company, and in such a manner that He was accused of being a glutton and a drunkard. The Son of God went to a village wedding. Not only did He attend, He worked a miracle so that the guests could have second servings of wine when the host's original supply failed. Surely He dressed as other men dressed if He was not easily recognized on many occasions. (He even had to be identified by Judas' kiss.) The one garment about which we are told must have been of the currently acceptable cut, or it is doubtful whether soldiers would have quibbled over it.

So if Jesus didn't seem to condemn worldly things themselves, why do we have the lists in Colossians and James of worldly things that are condemned? Let us be very careful to note that these do not list material things— they are characteristics of people, that is, they are specific sins. We are to put to death these worldly (or "earthly") things, since we have been raised from the dead with Christ Himself, and we no longer have any business with immorality, impurity, evil desire, covetousness, anger, malice, slander, foul talk, or lying. These spring from a desire for "things" that the world can provide, such as acclaim and status, or they attach themselves to material things in such a way that we may need to be stripped of the thing in order to repent of the sin.

He may be asking us to sell a much-loved house, to retire from a position in which we feel ourselves irreplaceable, to turn over to Him fears which hold us in bondage, to give up forms of self-improvement or recreation or social life which hinder obedience. Afterwards, with a joyful lightness of spirit and awareness of God's active involvement in ordering our happiness, we may wonder why we waited so long.

The process of being stripped does not feel good. But the joy we taste is not incompatible with the sorrow. I remember waking up one morning in my house in Shandia after Jim had been killed. The bed was empty beside me. Suddenly, in the place of fresh tears of sorrow, I was surprised by a sudden, unexpected surge of joyful exultation, realizing where Jim was at that very moment. He would never have to suffer again. He would never have to undergo the degradations and humiliations of old age. I would never have to spend days and nights in that dreadful fear of not knowing if he was safe. He was now with the Lord. Even with the reality of my widowhood and my daughter's fatherlessness and the house and station that I had to run all by myself—there was joy! Psalm 116:17: "I will offer the sacrifices of thanksgiving."

I will offer Him both my tears and my exultation. Nothing we offer to Him will be lost. It is the person who tries to save him- or herself who loses it all. Jesus gave His word: "Whoever loses his life for my sake will find it" (Matthew 10:39, NIV).

Indeed I also count all things loss for the excellence of the knowledge of Christ Jesus my Lord, for whom I have suffered the loss of all things, and count them as rubbish, that I may gain Christ and be found in Him, not having my own righteousness, which is from the law, but that which is through faith in Christ, the righteousness which is from God by faith;

that I may know Him and the power of His resur-
rection and the fellowship of His sufferings, being
conformed to His death.

PHILIPPIANS 3:8-10

Knocking Out the Props

It is an unsettling business, this being made conformable to His death, and it cannot be accomplished without knocking out the props. If we understand that God is at work even when He knocks out the small props, it will be easier for us to take it when He knocks out bigger ones.

The very week which I had looked forward to to begin the writing of a book found me dragging around with what appeared to be a heavy cold, accompanied by a deep cough. I tried to work at my accustomed place and pace. I couldn't. I could not grasp a thought, hold onto it firmly, and carry it through to its logical conclusion. A day or two went by with little to show. I took myself by the scruff of the neck—"Get on with it!"—but found that a prop had been knocked out. I had a fever. Only a degree or two, but enough to scramble my brains, and a salutary reminder that normal health and the ability to do ordinary work are gifts from God for which I should thank Him every day of my life. A letter "happened" (was ordained) to come then, remarking that God is much more interested in making us holy than He is in getting a job done. The letter made me pause. The interruption was more important, for those few days, than the book.

I was reminded of St. Augustine's words, "The very pleasures of human life men acquire by difficulties." Sometimes we recognize them only in retrospect. On one of those terrible days during my second husband's cancer, when he could hardly bear the pain or the thought of yet another treatment, and I could hardly bear to bear it with him, we remarked on how wonderful it would be to have just a single *ordinary* day.

And then there are the inevitabilities of old age. Wear and tear make their indelible marks on our face reflected in the mirror which (weirdly and shockingly sometimes) becomes the face of a stranger. Fear overtakes us as we take note of how much altered we have become, and we contemplate what is to come. The specters of loneliness, illness, abandonment, and the serial deprivation of our powers stare back at us from the furrowed and sagging face. But God will be there. There is no need to fear the future, *God is already there,* and God's promise for us is, "They still bring forth fruit in old age" (Psalm 92:14, RSV). The best fruit will be what is produced by the best-pruned branch.

More, and Then Some

I will offer Him my prayers, my sighs. I will pour out my heart to Him. Even in their distractedness, inconsistency, and deficiency, I can be confident that my prayers rise to Him like incense ("Let my prayer be counted as incense before thee, and the lifting up of my hands as an evening sacrifice!" Psalm 141:2, RSV). He receives my imperfect prayers like the mother receives the crushed dandelions, as gifts made perfect in love. Besides, He Himself has been praying for *me* all along: "He is able to save completely those who come to God through him, because he always lives to intercede for them" (Hebrews 7:25, NIV).

What else can I offer Him? In the words of Isaac Watts' great hymn, "When I Survey the Wondrous Cross":

Were the whole realm of nature mine,
That were an offering far too small;
Love so amazing, so divine,
Demands my soul, my life, my all.

My all, to gain all.

The widow of Zarephath (1 Kings 17) was destitute, even more desperate than the ordinary widow of the time because those were days of famine. Along comes Elijah, who had been getting supplied with bread and meat morning and evening courtesy of divinely ordered ravens, but who had left when the brook dried up from the drought. The ravens did not come with him to Zarephath. When he came to the town gate, he saw the woman gathering sticks.

> He called to her and asked, "Would you bring me a little water in a jar so I may have a drink?" As she was going to get it, he called, "And bring me, please a piece of bread."
> "As surely as the Lord your God lives," she replied, "I don't have any bread—only a handful of flour in a jar and a little oil in a jug. I am gathering a few sticks to take home and make a meal for myself and my son, that we may eat it—and die."
> 1 KINGS 17:11-12, NIV

The widow was a most unlikely prospect to provide for his needs. But the prophet Elijah prevailed upon her, and she believed him when he spoke, "For this is what the Lord, the God of Israel, says: 'The jar of flour will not be used up and the jug of oil will not run dry until the day the Lord gives rain on the land'" (1 Kings 17:14).

The nameless widow used up all her flour and oil and

made him bread, giving her all, and the word came true. The same God who ordered for Elijah more than was on the menu will do the same for us, if we are listening when He asks us for some small, but usually very important, sacrifice.

🌿Two🌿

*A*cceptance and Peace

I sat next to a lady at a luncheon once who told me that she and her husband had learned he had an incurable and very slowly debilitating disease when they had been married for only a very short time. She said, "When we got home, we sat down together and asked what we were going to do. We decided that we could be miserable for twenty-five years, or however long it would last, or we could be happy. And we chose to be happy." She added, "We had twenty-five wonderful years before he died."

Another time, as I sat at the book table following a seminar, a lady cut through the line, dropped a letter into my lap, and said, "You can read this if you want to, or just throw it away," and quickly disappeared. I hardly had time to see her face, but of course I read her letter and my heart went out to her. She said her name was June and she wrote that she is a committed Christian, Sunday school superintendent, witness to neighbors and friends, seamstress, homemaker, mother of three. The story she told is not a new one:

"Please, can you help me to understand what I must do? I do not love or respect my husband." She described him—

Christian, church elder, honor graduate, successful businessman. "We appear to be the ideal couple but I am dreadfully unhappy in our thirty-year marriage." She went on. "Bill has been emotionally crippled since his unhappy childhood and he does not share intimately, though I have loved him for years and years. My hurt is so deep."

What should June do? The situation seems unique to her, but it's certainly not the first time God has seen it. His promise is there in the Book—a promise for help and strength. "I will never leave you nor forsake you." But we have to come to Him in humility, acknowledging our helplessness and our utter dependence on Him, not hanging onto our expectations. I wonder if June is (I wonder if *I* am) asking of a man more than he can give?

Let's assume that June has prayed faithfully, pleaded earnestly, and tried every way in the world to draw Bill out of his incommunicative shell. What makes June extremely unhappy might not faze another woman, but never mind that. The Lord knows the frame of each of us, our hopes and disappointments, and *He has promised that our suffering will one day turn into glory if we'll respond to it in faith and obedience.* That's the actual crux of the matter.

First, we can rest assured that the situation in which we find ourselves (and nowhere else) is the very place where God wants to meet us. It is here that we will grow into the likeness of Christ. So this means that the suffering itself is not meaningless, it is not "for nothing." It is an element in God's loving purpose.

June's unhappiness, I believe, springs not from her husband's failures and limitations, but from her failure to accept him as he is. He is God's gift to her.

She had certain expectations of what a husband ought to be and do for his wife, some of them realistic, some unrealistic. So has every wife (and husband). But to truly love means to give yourself for others. To give yourself entails accepting disappointment and laying yourself open to suffering. To suffer—if you do so in the close company of Christ—means ultimately to reign with Him. June has the perfect chance to do all of the above, without too much temptation to do it only for what she'll get out of it here and now.

I would like to tell June to give thanks to God for this man. God perfectly understands his past, his inability to share intimately, and his refusal to accept responsibility for it. That's between Bill and God. God isn't going to hold her responsible for what Bill didn't do. She is not, in other words, his moral custodian. Her job is to love him, to do everything she would do if she were madly in love with him.

Work at it, June. Do it cheerfully, as unto the Lord. Maybe the Lord will change both of you through this. Maybe He won't. But when you see His face I think He will say, "Well done, good and faithful servant. Enter into the joy of your Master!" It will be worth it then. (I'm pretty sure you'll find out, long before then, that it's worth it *now*—if you do it with thanksgiving and gladness, as unto the Lord.) God never does anything *to* us that isn't *for* us.

Accepting With Both Hands

Amy Carmichael wrote a poem she called "In Acceptance Lieth Peace." That phrase has become a dictum for me. Acceptance of my circumstances, the first step in obtaining joy and peace, begins with faith. I would have no reason simply to accept the awful things that happen if I had no idea that Somebody was governing this world and that my individual life was completely under the control of One who possesses perfect wisdom, perfect justice, and perfect love.

We have to ask ourselves repeatedly, especially when the temptations and the dark times come, "Do I really believe this? Do I still believe this? Can I hang my soul on this? Do I really believe that God is governing this world and everything that touches me with perfect wisdom, justice, and love?" He who keeps us neither slumbers nor sleeps. His love is always awake, always aware, always surrounding and upholding and protecting. If a spear or a bullet finds its target in the flesh of one of His servants, it is not because of inattention on His part. It is because of love.

If His lordship is really established over me, it makes no difference (I might even say it's "no big deal") whether I live or die. I am expendable. That knowledge is freedom. I have no care for anything, for all that I am, all that I have, all that I do, and all that I suffer have been joyfully placed at His disposal.

The faith of Job on his ash-heap is astounding in view of how much less he knew of the love of God than we who know Him through the life and death of Jesus Christ. We have a whole Bible full of revelations about suffering. Job's response was perhaps closer to capitulation than acceptance, but it was enough. God told his friends Job had spoken the truth about Him while they had not.

We have been shown the way of acceptance on every page of the life of Jesus. It sprang from love and from trust. He set His face like a flint toward Jerusalem. He took up the cross of His own will. No one could take His life from Him. He deliberately laid it down. He calls us to take up our crosses. That is a different thing from capitulation or resignation. It is a glad and voluntary YES to the conditions we meet on our journey with Him, because these are the conditions He wants us to share with Him. Events are the *sacraments* of the Will of God—that is, they are visible signs of an invisible Reality. These provide the very place where we may learn to love and trust. Heaven waits for our response.

God included the hardships of my life in His original plan. Nothing takes Him by surprise. Nothing is for nothing. His plan is to make me holy, and hardship is indispensable for that as long as I live in this hard old world. All I have to do is accept it.

Three eternal and unshakable verities were what held me and comforted me during the terminal illness of my second husband, Add. I told myself the truth: Christ has died, Christ has risen, Christ will come again. Nothing can undermine those facts. Surely it was those truths that sustained the faithful disciple John when he was exiled to the island of Patmos. He was sustained by his faith, and he saw…

… seven golden lampstands, and among the lamp-stands was someone "like the Son of man," dressed in a robe reaching down to his feet and with a golden sash around his chest. His head and hair were white like wool, as white as snow, and his eyes were like blazing fire. His feet were like bronze glowing in a furnace, and his voice was like the sound of rushing waters. In his right hand he held seven stars, and out of his mouth came a sharp double-edged sword. His

face was like the sun shining in all its brilliance.
When I saw him, I fell at his feet as though dead.
Then he placed his right hand, the one that held the
seven stars, upon me and said: "Do not be afraid; I
am the First and the Last. I am the Living One; I was
dead, and behold I am alive for ever and ever! And I
hold the keys of death and Hades."

REVELATION 1:12-18, NIV

The One who has the keys is the One who is in charge. And if we have given our lives to Him, we are able to accept everything that happens to us as from His hands.

John was not out of the will of God by being in that place of suffering and exile and probably great loneliness. Presumably he was an elderly man at that time, undoubtedly experiencing the weaknesses and the limitations of old age. But if the least thing could happen to him without God's permission and sustaining grace, it would mean something was out of God's control, which would contradict the unshakable fact that He is, above all and for all time, in charge.

Waiting Rooms

Sometimes it is hardest to accept the *waiting* parts of life. I think of the story told by Amy Carmichael in her first year of missionary work in Japan. She and a missionary couple were delayed on a journey because of a boat that did not arrive. Not just hours but days went by, and the young missionary began to fret because of the time lost and the consequences to others who counted on them. The older missionary said calmly, "God knows all about the boats." It became a maxim of faith for the rest of her life.

Many times in my life God has asked me to wait when I wanted to move forward. He has kept me in the dark when I asked for light. I like to see progress. I look for evidence that God is at least doing something. If the Shepherd leads us beside still waters when we were hoping for whitewater excitement, it is hard to believe anything really vital is taking place. God is silent. The house is silent. The phone doesn't ring. The mailbox is empty. The stillness is hard to bear—and God knows that. He knows our frame and remembers we are made of dust. He is very patient with us when we are trying to be patient with Him. Of course for most of us this test of waiting does not take place in a silent and empty house, but in the course of regular work and appointments and taxpaying and grocery buying and trying to have the car fixed and get the storm windows up; daily decisions have to go on being made, responsibilities fulfilled, families provided for, employers satisfied. Can we accept the patience-taxing ordinary things alongside the four-alarm fires of our lives?

Psalm 16:5 is one of my life verses now. "Lord, you have assigned me my portion and my cup and have made my lot secure." My "lot" is what happens to me—my share of that which comes by the will of the Power that rules my destiny. My lot includes the circumstances of my birth, my upbringing, my job, my hardships, the people I work with, my marital status, hindrances, obstacles, accidents, and opportunities. Everything constitutes my lot. Nothing excepted. If I can accept that fact at every turn in the road, I have indeed stepped into His everlasting arms even more securely, and there I will find peace and joy.

Disasters

Remember what happened to Mary and Martha. Their brother died. He had been their sole support. Jesus came too late. The account reads as follows (John 11:5-6, 21, 32, 15, NIV): "Jesus loved Martha and her sister and Lazarus. Yet when he heard that Lazarus was sick, he stayed where he was two more days." How strange.

When He finally arrived, of course both Mary and Martha were in despair and grief. They each said the same thing to Him, "Lord, if you had been here, my brother would not have died." And He said, "I am glad that I was not there, so that you may believe." What could they make of that? He could have healed him easily, but He let him die. He allowed a disaster to occur.

He had in store something inestimably more wonderful than what they had wished for, something they had never dreamed possible.

I think that He does that with us quite often. Our major problems of acceptance and trust usually have to do with timing, because God's timetable is always different from ours. He wants me to wait in order to believe, in order to learn to put my faith in His timing.

The same God who raised Lazarus is the One who is in charge of our lives. With that in mind, we can accept whatever comes from His hand, trusting that He means it for our good. We can each look back in our lives and see the things that would not have happened if something else hadn't happened. It may have been a disaster, but think about the ways in which God has worked since then.

The deepest spiritual lessons come through suffering. It takes the deep water and the hot fire and the dark valley to teach us the walk of faith. I would not be able to state this with such authority if it were not for losing my first husband Jim. That shattering event precipitated a lifetime of learning rich spiritual lessons, writing and speaking about what I have learned, and holding on in ever-increasing faith to the One who will one day receive me into His presence. The verse that came to mind when I received the shortwave message that Jim was missing was Isaiah 43:2: "When thou passeth through the waters, I will

be with thee, and through the rivers, they shall not over-
flow thee; when thou walkest through the fire, thou shalt
not be burned. Neither shall the flame kindle upon thee.
For I am the Lord thy God." I can testify that He has never
broken that promise. He kept those words through those
five agonizing days while we five wives waited to discover
whether our husbands were indeed dead or alive. He kept
me through all the subsequent years. He didn't give me a
bridge over troubled waters, but He kept the promise that
when I passed through the waters, He would be with me.
His promise applies to each of us. The one thing that He
requires of us in response to deep waters is *acceptance.*
This acceptance is not passivism, quietism, fatalism, or
resignation. Peace and joy and faith will not be found in
forgetting, and they will not be found in busyness or
aloofness or the submission of defeat. They will not be
found in anger at the "unfairness" of it all. St. Francis de
Sales said, "Accustom yourself to unreasonableness and
injustice! God sees these things far better than you do, *and
permits them!*"

Once there was a lady in our church who was like a
tigress in a corner. She lashed out with all claws bared at
everybody. All I knew about her was that she was a widow,
as I was also. I didn't know whether that was what was
eating her or whether it was something else, perhaps a great
evil perpetrated against her by someone, but it was very

obvious that she had never accepted *something* in her life.

There wasn't anything anyone could do to get near that woman and comfort her. She destroyed every small group she ever joined and disrupted all kinds of things in that church. One night at a church supper, I happened to be seated opposite her. She got up to get a cup of coffee, and when she came back, the sweet girl who was waiting on tables had taken away her dessert plate that still had about two bites of her pie left on it. The lady exclaimed, "Who took my pie! Where's my pie!"

I said, "The girl who's serving tables."

So she called the girl over and remonstrated, "Where's my piece of pie?"

The girl apologized, "Oh, I'm so sorry. I thought you were finished. I will get you another piece of pie."

"I don't want another piece of pie. I want *that* piece of pie. I want those two bites."

That's the way she was with everybody. She came late to my house one night for a committee meeting and burst through the door without any preliminaries saying, "Nobody told me what time this thing was; I had a terrible time finding this place; I don't know what's the matter with you people...." I don't know where that poor lady is now. She left our church a long time ago. Perhaps she has now learned acceptance.

Get to the Root

If we can identify the source of what rankles us, we are halfway to accepting our difficulties with faith. Here are the most common sources of our hard-to-accept problems:

Other people. Those who annoy and trouble us are part of our assigned portion and lot. God makes the assignments, and He apportions the degree of difficulty in precise measurements.

Accidents. Disasters put us in a quandary. We don't see how things can ever work out. But God says, "You are loved with an everlasting love" (Jeremiah 31:3) and "underneath are the everlasting arms" (Deuteronomy 33:27). He will never let us down if we stay with Him.

Limitations. We would prefer to have the exalted spiritual experiences or God-given gifts that He has given to somebody else. We tend to settle into our corner thinking, "I must have been behind the door when God gave out gifts, so I can never live as well as that fortunate person." But we can offer our limitations, like widow's mites, to Him. "Blessed are those who hear the Word of God and do it" (Luke 11:27-28).

Choose Your Weapon

If true acceptance means we acknowledge that the Lord of the universe is the Lord of this current trouble of ours, and if acceptance is the first step toward peace, how can we achieve it? Here are six choices that lead to acceptance:

Choose your attitude. We read in 2 Corinthians 12:10, "For Christ's sake I delight in weaknesses, in insults, in hardships, in persecutions, in difficulties." Does that come naturally? Of course not. But you can *choose* to delight in weaknesses. "For when I am weak, then I am strong." This is one of the magnificent paradoxes of the cross: You bring to the cross your weakness and you receive God's strength. You bring Him your sins and you receive His righteousness. You bring Him your sorrows and you receive His joy. You can choose to trust His faithfulness in every detail of your life and, in turn, that choice enables you to delight in the same messy details that could have dismayed you.

Choose to offer your pain to God. Whatever you are offering—pain, heartbreak, suffering, an accident, any disaster—you know you cannot handle it yourself. You don't need to go to thirty-nine of your closest friends first. The first thing you should do before crying on anybody's shoulder is to open your hands and lift up your pain to

God. He knows how to bring good out of evil. You may need to repeat this offering many times.

Choose to receive what God has given with open hands. Receive this thing that you cannot change. It is a willed choice. This thing that has happened for you, down to the least circumstance, is the will of God. E.B. Pusey wrote:

> This, then, is faith, that everything, the very least, or what seems to us great, every change of the seasons, everything which touches us in mind, body, or estate, whether brought about through this outward sense-less nature, or by the will of man, good or bad, is overruled to each of us by the all-holy and all-loving will of God. Whatever befalls us, however it befalls us, we must receive as the Will of God. If it befalls us through man's negligence, or ill-will, or anger, still it is, in even the least circumstance, to us the will of God. For if the least thing could happen to us without God's permission, it would be something out of God's control. God's providence or His love would not be what they are. Almighty God Himself would not be the same God; not the God Whom we believe, adore, and love.

Choose to renew your commitment to Him. He does know what He is doing. The psalmist said, "When I am afraid, I will trust in you" (Psalm 56:3-4, NIV). In the same verse we note both emotion ("When I am afraid") and willpower ("I will trust"). In spite of your emotional state, you can choose Him once again.

Choose to praise Him as Habakkuk did. Habakkuk praised God when there were no figs on the tree, no grapes on the vine, no cattle in the stall. Habakkuk didn't feel good about having no figs, no grapes, and no cattle, but he chose to rejoice in the Lord. You don't have to paste on a happy smile and pretend to be tickled to death because something dreadful has happened, but you surely can rejoice. Christ has died, Christ has risen, Christ will come again.

Choose to do the next thing. "Do the Next Thing" has become one of the mottoes of my life. I am indebted to an unknown author for the following verses:

> From an old English parsonage, down by the sea
> There came in the twilight a message to me;
> Its quaint Saxon legend, deeply engraven,
> Hath, as it seems to me, teaching from Heaven.
> And on through the hours the quiet words ring

Like a low inspiration—
"DO THE NEXT THING."

Many a questioning, many a fear,
Many a doubt, hath its quieting here.
Moment by moment, let down from Heaven,
Time, opportunity, guidance, are given.
Fear not tomorrows, Child of the King,
Trust them with Jesus,
"DO THE NEXT THING."

Do it immediately; do it with prayer;
Do it reliantly, casting all care;
Do it with reverence, tracing His Hand
Who placed it before thee with earnest command.
Stayed on Omnipotence, safe 'neath His wing,
Leave all resultings,
"DO THE NEXT THING."

Looking to Jesus, ever serener,
(Working or suffering) be thy demeanor,
In His dear presence, the rest of His calm,
The light of His countenance be thy psalm,
Strong in His faithfulness, praise and sing,
Then, as He beckons thee
"DO THE NEXT THING."

There is nothing magical about any of this. The Lord has assigned you your portion and your cup; it is designated, measured precisely. Are you upset because you have been hindered from doing what you wanted to do, or perhaps what you thought God wanted you to do? Jesus Christ provides the way out of the labyrinth of the world into the freedom of the new creation. You will keep the same talents, the same circumstances, the same health, the same family, the same property, the same daily demands. But as someone has said, "A door has opened, and the crossing over to Christ has been made possible by acceptance." In Acceptance Lieth Peace.

❦ Three ❦

All Things Are Yours

The longer I live, the more fully I become convinced that the Lord is in charge of *everything* on this complicated Earth and that nothing happens without His permission. It's one of the great advantages of old age to be so completely sure of that. God Almighty is *sovereign*. He is the One who is paramount, autonomous, unlimited, supreme, all-loving, the absolute ruler of everything.

It seems to me that our modern church life, with its emphasis on cozy friendship with God, has deprived us somewhat of an awe-filled appreciation for His sovereignty. It's not that we take issue with it, exactly. We recognize His hand at work at startling or spectacular moments. We extol His power to save when He has just protected us from a car accident, we marvel at His glory when we visit the Grand Canyon, and we remember the mysteries of His ways when somebody dies. However, as we plod through the ordinary middle ground of our lives, the long distances between the punctuation marks of exultation and desolation, we fail to appreciate God's sovereignty. We find it particularly hard to comprehend, much less believe, that a good God could still be in charge when our ordinary life is a relentless string of difficulties or when disasters strike.

He is "Most High over the earth" (Psalm 83:18). He is most high over our ordinary muddles and He is most high over what may seem to be catastrophes. He is most high over international affairs and global warming and all the human squabbles that have ever cropped up. He is in charge of destruction and He is in charge of salvation.

Notice verse 28 in the fourth chapter of the Book of Acts (in italics below):

On their release, Peter and John went back to their own people and reported all that the chief priests and elders had said to them. When they heard this, they raised their voices together in prayer to God. "Sovereign Lord," they said, "you made the heaven and the earth and the sea, and everything in them. You spoke by the Holy Spirit through the mouth of your servant, our father David:

"'Why do the nations rage
    and the peoples plot in vain?
The kings of the earth take their stand
    and the rulers gather together
against the Lord
    and against his Anointed One.'

Indeed Herod and Pontius Pilate met together with
the Gentiles and the people of Israel in this city to
conspire against your holy servant Jesus, whom you
anointed. *They did what your power and will had
decided beforehand should happen."*

Acts 4:23-28, NIV, emphasis mine

Those wicked men—Herod and Pontius Pilate and the
others who had raged against Jesus and who were now
trying to eliminate His followers—how could they be
doing only what God's "power and will had decided
beforehand should happen"? Does that mean that God
was in favor of such things?

Were Jesus' followers in favor of these things? How
were they praying about them? They didn't try to fathom
the fine points, it seems. They simply wanted to cooperate
with the rest of God's plan. Instead of saying, "Lord, please
make them quit acting like this," they were so certain of
God's involvement that their only prayer was, "Consider
their threats and enable your servants to speak your word
with great boldness" (v. 29). That must have been the right
prayer for the situation because "after they prayed, the
place where they were meeting was shaken. And they
were all filled with the Holy Spirit and spoke the word of
God boldly" (v. 31).

Most of the time, we cannot figure out what good thing

God is going to bring out of what happens. His plan is bigger. He may or He may not adjust it for our personal comfort. Evelyn Underhill said, "If God were small enough to be understood, He wouldn't be big enough to be worshiped."

If you were God, would you have asked the good man Noah to spend years building a ship on dry land, making him the laughingstock of the neighborhood? Would you have created a Goliath? Would you, without reassuring him that he would not be harmed, have allowed your dedicated servant Daniel to be thrown into a pit full of ravenous lions? Even with the benefit of hindsight, it's difficult to articulate the justification for such plans.

"All the paths of the Lord are lovingkindness and truth to those who keep His covenant and His testimonies" (Psalm 25:10, NASB). About this passage, Amy Carmichael once wrote in a note to a coworker, "*All* does not mean 'all but these paths we are in now' or 'nearly all, but perhaps not just this specially difficult painful one.' All must mean *all*."

Caused or Allowed?

"This man" (speaking of Jesus) "was handed over to you by God's set purpose and foreknowledge; and you, with the help of wicked men, put him to death by nailing him to the cross" (Acts 2:23, NIV). This was the worst thing that had ever happened in human history and God didn't stop it. Instead, He transfigured it into the best thing that ever happened, securing the salvation of the human race. Having planned it all ahead of time, the sovereign God used the hands and whips of wicked men to punish and kill His own Son.

God was not asleep when John the Baptist got his head chopped off. His attention was not deflected when Stephen was stoned to death. God was still in heaven when His Son was nailed to the cross. Jesus Himself knew what was going to happen to Him. He agonized in the garden over His approaching death. He had not, however, worked His way through the five stages of grief. Instead, He showed us the shortcut to peace, which is acceptance. He acquiesced, trustingly, to the will of His Father.

To those of us who are not theologians, does it matter whether a thing is *ordained* or merely *allowed?* Are events that seem to be out of control caused by God? Or does He allow them to occur at the hands of human beings? You can spend a lot of time pondering that one and end up pretty much where you started. In either case, the purpose remains the same—our sanctification. God is in the business of making us walking, breathing examples of the invisible reality of the presence of Christ in us.

From the very beginning God decided that those who came to him—and all along he knew who would—should become like his Son, so that his Son would be the First, with many brothers. And having chosen us, he called us to come to him; and when we came, he declared us "not guilty," filled us with Christ's goodness, gave us right standing with himself, and promised us his glory.

ROMANS 8:29-30, LB

We who have given ourselves to Him have given up our "right" to call the shots. It wasn't much of a right in the first place, since we are incapable of effecting very many changes to our life situation. We have also given up our right to squawk about difficulties. Paul realized early on that his "thorn in the flesh" was not going to go away even if he asked nicely. He didn't object to the idea that God, in order to keep him humble, would allow the devil himself to send an affliction.

Because of the surpassing greatness of the revelations, for this reason, to keep me from exalting myself, *there was given me a thorn in the flesh, a messenger of Satan to torment me*—to keep me from exalting myself! Concerning this I implored the Lord three times that it might leave me. And He has said to me,

"My grace is sufficient for you, for power is perfected in weakness." Most gladly, therefore, I will rather boast about my weaknesses, so that the power of Christ may dwell in me.

2 CORINTHIANS 12:13-19, NASB, emphasis mine

Our Response

I need frequent reminders that God does not allow anything to occur that will prevent me from doing His will. Absolutely nothing can interfere with His plans, and what may look to me like Plan B (or Z) is Plan A all along. When Paul and Peter were imprisoned, did that prevent them from doing the will of God? Peter wrote to God's elect, who were still God's elect even though they were in exile:

Peter, an apostle of Jesus Christ, To those who reside as aliens, scattered throughout Pontus, Galatia, Cappadocia, Asia, and Bithynia, who are chosen according to the foreknowledge of God the Father, by the sanctifying work of the Spirit, that you may obey Jesus Christ and be sprinkled with His blood: May grace and peace be yours in the fullest measure. Blessed be the God and Father of our Lord Jesus Christ, who according to His great mercy has caused us to be born again to a living hope through the resurrection of Jesus Christ from the dead, to obtain an

*inheritance which is imperishable and undefiled and
will not fade away, reserved in heaven for you, who
are protected by the power of God through faith for
a salvation ready to be revealed in the last time.*

1 PETER 1:1-5, NIV

Peter wanted the recipients of his letter to remember
what's important, namely that they have been claimed by
the sovereign God, who will be sure to see them through
thick and thin, and that their true inheritance cannot be
wrested away from them as their earthly possessions
probably were.

Although our tests and trials may be different ones, we
have the same inheritance that they did. The plan of God
for our lives includes *all* of our circumstances, our entire
heredity, every detail of our environment, each decision
we make, all the decisions of others, absolutely everything. He can make even the wrath of man to praise
Him—or any discomfiting circumstance.

For Mark Twain in the winter of 1887, it was bad
weather. He had anticipated a getaway with his wife Livy,
who would come to him in New York from Hartford,
Connecticut and then go with him for a brief holiday in
Washington:

And so, after all my labor and persuasion to get you to at last promise to take a week's holiday and go off with me on a lark, this is what Providence has gone and done about it. A mere simple *request* to you to stay at home would have been entirely sufficient: but no, that is not big enough, picturesque enough—a blizzard's the idea: pour down all the snow in stock, turn loose all the winds, bring a whole continent to a stand-still: that is Providence's idea of the correct way to trump a person's trick. Dear me, if I had known it was going to make all this trouble and cost all these millions, I never would have said anything *about* your going to Washington.*

Our perspective is so limited. We keep forgetting that God's love does not show itself only in protection from suffering. It is of a different nature altogether. His love does not hate tragedy. It never denies reality. It stands firm in the teeth of suffering. The love of God did not protect His own Son from death on a cross. That was the proof of His love, though "legions of angels" might have rescued Him. He will not necessarily protect us—not from anything it takes to make us like Jesus. A lot of hammering and chiseling and purifying by fire will have to go into the

*Edith Colgate Salabury, *Susy and Mark Twain* (New York: Harper and Row, 1965), 249–50.

process. Through it all, we learn to trust Him in every little thing.

Waiting on God

Sometimes the deepest level of trust has the appearance of doing nothing. This does not go down well with our busy souls.

I have a collection of books written by my grandfather. In one of them, *When Days Seem Dark*, I came across these words:

Standing still, on some occasions, is the paramount duty of the follower of Christ. There are times when we must be merely onlookers, when the flesh and the brain refuse to work, hopes shrivel like autumn leaves and we simply do not know which way to turn. It may be just then that we shall learn for the first time how to stand still in perfect peace and quietness of soul, not idling away our time, not hopelessly limp and heedless of the outcome, but working on in such ways as may be given to us, observing with eager joy the way in which God will work it all out to a perfectly glorious ending.

All our little fussiness and haste, all our strong anxiety and warping care are as futile as the tugging of a little child's hand at the great iron knob of a closed and barred gate through which his loving father does not care to have him go just then.

One of my favorite verses, one that my mother gave me many years ago, was Naomi's answer to Ruth, "Sit still, my daughter, until thou know how the matter will fall" (Ruth 3:18, KJV). The Lord had given my mother that verse when she was worried about the possibility of being a foreign missionary. She thought it would be perfectly dreadful if the Lord should call her to be a missionary. But she obeyed. She "sat still" and she found His peace, which made her equally willing to go to Belgium as a missionary for a few years, and then to return to the United States to live out her life as a housewife, a friend of missionaries, and a mother of missionaries.

Our response is what matters. A quiet heart is content with what God gives. It is enough. All is grace. One morning my computer simply would not obey me. What a nuisance. I had my work laid out, my timing figured, my mind all set. My work was delayed, my timing thrown off, my thinking interrupted. Then I remembered. It was not for nothing. This was part of the Plan (not mine, His). "Lord, You have assigned me my portion and my cup."

Now if the interruption had been a human being instead of an infuriating mechanism, it would not have been so hard to see it as the most important part of the work of the day. But *all* is under my Father's control: yes, recalcitrant computers, faulty transmissions, drawbridges that happen to be *up* when I am in a hurry. My portion. My cup. My lot is secure. My heart can be at peace. My Father is in charge. How simple!

My assignment entails my willing acceptance of my portion in matters far beyond comparison with the trivialities just mentioned, such as the death of a precious baby. A mother wrote to me of losing her son when he was just one month old. A widow wrote of the long agony of watching her husband die. The number of years given them in marriage seemed too few. We can know only that Eternal Love is wiser than we, and we bow in adoration of that loving wisdom.

Response is what matters. All events serve His will. Remember that our forefathers all were guided by the pillar of cloud, all passed through the sea, all ate and drank the same spiritual food and drink, but God was not pleased with most of them. Their responses were wrong. Bitter about the portions allotted to them, they indulged in idolatry, gluttony, and sexual sin. The same almighty God apportioned their experiences. Some responded in faith. Most did not.

God came down and lived in this world as a man. He showed us how to live in this world, subject to its vicissitudes and necessities, that we might be changed, not into angels or storybook princesses, not wafted into another world, but changed into saints in this world. The secret is Christ in me, not in a different set of circumstances.

❧Four❧

*M*aterial Evidence

Spiritual things are best understood through what we can see with our eyes, hear with our ears, taste with our tongues, smell with our noses, or hold in our hands. The Lord God, fully aware that our human limitations would keep us from knowing Him in all His glory, gives us all kinds of material evidence to show us what He and His kingdom are like. He knew we mere mortals would need help in order to "get it." If we pay attention, we can collect the evidence and find out more about Him—His creativity and omniscient omnipresence, His desire to save us from our sin, His ability to make us holy, and His eagerness to draw us to Himself. Such material evidence can be considered a *sacrament,* a word that means a visible sign of an invisible reality.

The word sacrament connotes mystery. Far from being only a genre of fiction, a mystery means anything beyond the possibility of full explanation. Why does God allow evil in the world? It's a mystery, something we can only make a stab at explaining. We need help with the mysteries of the Christian faith such as the Annunciation, the Incarnation, the Crucifixion, the Resurrection, and the

Ascension of Christ. These big words direct our attention to infinite and incomprehensible truths. Could any doctor explain the gynecology of the Virgin Birth? But we believe in it—by faith, which is the only way to apprehend such truths.

In the fifth chapter of Paul's letter to the Ephesians we read a very specific example of how an earthly representation helps us understand an invisible reality. Paul writes about how the marriage of a man and a woman represents the mystery of the union between Jesus Christ and the church, a union between God and humankind:

> *Wives, submit to your husbands as to the Lord. For the husband is the head of the wife as Christ is the head of the church, his body, of which he is the Savior. Now as the church submits to Christ, so also wives should submit to their husbands in everything.*
>
> *Husbands, love your wives, just as Christ loved the church and gave himself up for her to make her holy, cleansing her by the washing with water through the word, and to present her to himself as a radiant church, without stain or wrinkle or any other blemish, but holy and blameless. In this same way, husbands ought to love their wives as their own bodies. He who loves his wife loves himself. After*

all, no one ever hated his own body, but he feeds and
cares for it, just as Christ does the church—for we
are members of his body.

EPHESIANS 5:22-30, NIV

We who are married become actors in a mystery play. In
the Middle Ages, traveling troupes of actors went from village to village, setting up portable stages in the town
squares. The people were illiterate and could not have read
the Bible stories even if they had had Bibles (which they
did not), so the players acted them out. The visible characters, props, and actions, and the audible dialogue portrayed the invisible truths of the Christian faith.

In the mystery play of marriage, the characters have
already been cast, and they are not interchangeable. The
husband has been given the role of the head. It is not by his
choice (or the wife's) and it is not by his achievement or by
popular vote. The wife has *not* been given the role of the
head, anymore than the church has been given the position of Christ Himself. It has nothing to do with which
partner in the marriage is smarter or more spiritual. (Nor
does it have to do with Paul's personality quirks, by the
way.) Human marriage represents an eternal reality. It's
sacramental in the fullest sense of the word.

In churches where there is an offertory, another material

evidence of self-giving is being presented. When I put my money into the plate or basket, my simple gesture represents a visible sign of the offering of my entire self to God. My purse belongs to Him because the rest of me belongs to Him. He owns me. In a condensed form, my weekly donation to the body of Christ (the church) represents my acknowledgment that every day, every breath, and every hope of heaven come from Him and ought to be returned to Him, with gratitude.

Nature

Jesus, like all good teachers, knew that people would soon forget what He taught them unless He used memorable illustrations. Many of His lessons were taken from nature. To illustrate invisible truths, He used salt, light, wind, wheat, stones, fig trees, sheep, birds, and field flowers, to name a few. Gesturing toward the flock of sheep grazing in the distance, He illustrated His Father's persistent love.

If a man owns a hundred sheep, and one of them wanders away, will he not leave the ninety-nine on the hills and go to look for the one that wandered off? And if he finds it, I tell you the truth, he is happier about that one sheep than about the ninety-nine that did not wander off. In the same way your Father in heaven is not willing that any of these little ones should be lost.

MATTHEW 18:12-14, NIV

And why do you worry about clothes? See how the lilies of the field grow. They do not labor or spin. Yet I tell you that not even Solomon in all his splendor was dressed like one of these. If that is how God clothes the grass of the field, which is here today and tomorrow is thrown into the fire, will he not much more clothe you, O you of little faith?

MATTHEW 6:28-30, NIV

The Lord God made it all, and the world shows us His glory. Everything is interconnected. When we sing the words of the hymn, "Great is Thy Faithfulness," we remind ourselves of this:

> Summer and winter and springtime and harvest,
> Sun, moon, and stars in their courses above
> Join with all nature in manifold witness
> To thy great faithfulness, mercy, and love.

One example of how nature provides a "manifold witness" of God's care is the red crabs of Christmas Island, which I learned about from a nature program on television.

Christmas Island is about a thousand miles south of Hawaii. There are millions of red crabs living in the inner part of the island. At a certain time of year, the crabs migrate across the island to the shore to mate. The males swarm back home while the females wait a couple of weeks before depositing their eggs in the sea, following after the males to the interior of the island. During these mass migrations back and forth, the surface of the island looks like a moving red rug. The crabs know when to go and exactly what to do, even when they have never been there before. The baby crabs hatch in the ocean, so tiny and transparent that it is hard to see how they can navigate at all. They climb out of the ocean and start moving across the island. Each crab is an exquisite creation, equipped with retractable eyes that come out on stems and go back into eye cups. Lacking eyelids, red crabs have a limb equipped with a tiny brush, so they can stick their eyes out and polish them with the brush. After they retract their eyes, they use the brush to clean the rim of the eye cup. Who thought all that up?

If we have eyes to see, we can figure out a lot about the Creator. Even if I have never heard of a microscope or a telescope or the Discovery Channel, the evidence presented to my own senses tells me that His creative and sustaining abilities are limitless, that He is not only consistent but that He loves variety and the interplay of color, sound, and texture.

Events

It's not only the natural world that reveals God to us. The events around us, often mundane, sometimes horrific, can speak to us more clearly than any preacher. From them, we understand bedrock truths such as humility ("I am not the center of the universe"), neediness ("I cannot provide for myself. Other people will let me down. God will have to provide for me"), and response ("God is in charge and I will trust Him"). Whether we take a slice of our life—one day or one year—or the whole sweep of it, we can see the evidence that the Lord of Heaven allows just the right things to happen to us to make us steadfast and childlike in our trust.

The joy and sorrow we experience in the circumstances of our lives speak to us about mysteries of God's sovereignty that are only apprehended by a faith-filled acceptance of every incident. Evelyn Underhill wrote, "Events are the sacraments of the will of God."

Actions

Then there are the *actions* of our daily lives. Eating, for instance. The next time you sit down at the table, think about this: "I stand at the door and knock. If anyone hears my voice and opens the door, I will come in and eat with him, and he with me" (Revelation 3:20, NIV). You may be taking just another bite of meatloaf, but if you will look beyond the morsel on your fork, you will see a God who wants to invite Himself to dinner! He could easily break down your door and barge in on you, but He stands patiently knocking, waiting for you to open the door of your heart and invite Him in.

People

The people around us prove to be sacramental evidence of God's love as well. Whether they are Christians or not, they are all intricately and wonderfully made. There is no end to the variety: "red and yellow, black and white ..." They may be good people by human standards, honest, beautiful, and kind; or they may be depraved, ugly, and unscrupulous. Those of us who are Christians are meant to reflect God's love and light to everyone we meet, becoming ourselves part of His material evidence to the world.

The Bible is a series of stories about people. Each one has been included for a reason. Each vignette, whether it portrays an upstanding, godly person or a Judas, serves as a positive or a negative proof of the ways of God.

The Book of Job is one of the earliest human records we

have, and it is the story of a man confronting evil and God Himself. A living proof of a living faith was required, not only for Job's friends, but for unseen powers in high places. Job's suffering provided the context for a demonstration of trust. While the patience of Job is often spoken of, he has never impressed me as being particularly patient. I do see that he was particularly faithful, even though he did not have the New Testament to help him understand his plight. With little to go on, Job kept on talking to God. We may take heart from the way he bore his suffering. It was the necessary proof of the reality of his faith—to us, to his contemporaries, and to our enemy Satan.

Has anyone ever counted all the people, named and unnamed, who appear in the pages of the Bible? There are so many, all portrayed "warts and all," that one is forced to conclude that God wants to reveal Himself through the material evidence provided by human beings and their exploits.

Communion

Without entering into theological quibbles about the number of church-sanctioned sacraments or what to call them, let's explore the ramifications of one sacrament that we label Communion or the Eucharist, which is used in the churches of most believers. When we participate in Communion, we are looking at material evidence: bread and wine, which were commonplace ingredients in any meal in Jesus' day. Those visible items contain invisible worlds of significance concerning Jesus' crucified body and the blood He shed so that we might live eternally.

Depending on where the church is gathered, Communion is administered in a variety of ways, using various forms of bread and various types of wine. Some Christians use a loaf and tear pieces off it for each other, others help themselves to tiny crackers, still others wait for the priest to place thin wafers on their tongues. Some Christians use special wine made only for liturgical purposes, others use Welch's grape juice. Some use one common cup and others use little individual ones. What makes it a sacrament isn't the specific items but the meaning behind them.

When I was a missionary in the jungle, there was no such thing as bread or wine. There were no ovens, no wheat, no grapes. The equivalent of bread to the Indians was manioc, which is a starchy tuber that is shaped like a carrot, with a brown skin, white on the inside. It is capable of being cooked in as many ways as potatoes, although it comes out stringy, heavy, rather gluey. It tastes better than it sounds to Westerners. Since it was the staple food of the Indians, manioc was generally what we used for the Lord's Supper. It was to them what bread is to us, and it was as different from the bread of Jesus' time as ours is.

Because the Indians had nothing even remotely resembling wine, we used whatever we could find. (I remember one time when the cup actually contained, by an innocent mistake, shellac. It went all the way around the circle with everyone taking a sip from the same cup, grimacing. It didn't hurt us, and it surely gave new meaning to Christ's bitter sacrifice!)

The breaking of the communion bread itself, whether done between fingers or teeth or both, is loaded with meaning, the sign of divine, self-giving love. If we take it a step further, we realize that we ourselves, Jesus' physical representatives here on earth, are meant to be broken bread, lovingly sacrificing our time and energy and substance daily for the sake of others.

"Reading" the material evidence is almost like learning a new language. The important thing is to pay attention to it. Let's learn to open our eyes and ears, taste the bread and wine, touch our child's fingertips. Let's not waste or trivialize such sacramental moments.

For since the creation of the world God's invisible qualities—his eternal power and divine nature—have been clearly seen, being understood from what has been made, so that men are without excuse.

ROMANS 1:20, NIV

He is the reflection of God's glory and the exact imprint of God's very being, and he sustains all things by his powerful word.

HEBREWS 1:3, NRSV

But we all, with unveiled face beholding as in a mirror the glory of the Lord, are being transformed into the same image from glory to glory, just as from the Lord, the Spirit.

2 CORINTHIANS 3:18, NASB

❧ Five ❧

*H*elps to Holiness

Is it more difficult to live a holy life in the twenty-first century than it was in the first century A.D. or in the 1890s? Many Christians would have us think so. The assumption seems to be that our century is rife with new pitfalls. In spite of the fact that holiness entails a certain amount of attention to particulars, which can vary enormously from one era or culture to another, it boils down to two foundational underpinnings that hold true for every century: Trust and Obey. Holiness means loving God and doing what He says. The first-century heart is the same as the twenty-first-century heart—desperately in need of saving, stubbornly selfish—and fairly disinclined to trust and obey God.

It's easy to see why we believe our path to holiness is more difficult than that of earlier or simpler Christians. Here we are, weltering in a plethora of choices, overloaded with information, stymied by our energy-saving devices, with too many places to go, too many things to do, too many choices all the time.

Recently, I was standing in a long line waiting to pay for an item of clothing. I turned to the man behind me and said, "You know the problem with America is that there are too many choices."

He said, "You're right. Too many choices. My wife works in a grocery store and there is a whole aisle of different breakfast cereals—nothing else in that aisle. That's where you see these frantic mothers with a two-year-old grabbing their skirts and an infant in the cart and a four-year-old racing toward the candy counter while the mother is saying to him (probably somewhat plaintively), 'Honey, what would you like for breakfast?'"

Our queue went back into a display of black dresses—black dresses as far as we could see. Now in the back of my mind I had been thinking that it would be rather nice to own a black dress. That is, until I saw that dizzying array of styles of black dresses!

Too many choices, too little time—but the same human heart reaching up to the same God who says "Be holy, because I am holy" (1 Peter 1:16). Peter is addressing Christians, those who bear the name of Christ, and he is backing up his imperative (do it!) by quoting the Book of Leviticus. Jesus Christ is the same yesterday and today and forever. He sees everything in your world and He wants you to listen to Him, trust Him, obey what He tells you to do.

❦

Deliver Us From Temptation

Is there a way of life, a manner of serving the Lord, that will deliver us from the temptations and distractions around us? Life in a convent or monastery looks to many of us on the outside as though it would almost guarantee a degree of holiness that is far beyond the rest of us. But a letter from a friend who is a nun showed me that there is no such guarantee. For her, as for me, to walk with God is to walk by faith, to trust and obey one day at a time, recognizing our never-ending need for grace:

> Elisabeth, every part of our "Rule" has been chosen to free us for prayer. Centuries of experience have contributed to providing us with an atmosphere most conducive to freeing the mind and heart for prayer. Yet I'm afraid with all that has been given, one can settle for the shell, going through the motions only. We can compromise the spirit of freedom we have received from the Lord Jesus with the ersatz security and satisfaction of bondage to the letter of our Rule. We can still very easily get caught up in the busy-ness that makes our heart more a marketplace than a

house of prayer.

I joined the Sisters upon my graduation from college. I'm afraid my decision was far from noble and generous. I didn't realize it at the time, but it was pretty much pride that led me here, the desire to excel, to do the most, the best. My temperament tended to approach things "from the chin up," and this decision, as I came to see later, was much more one of my mind than of my heart. That's where I was "at," and from that place the Lord drew me, in spite of my faults and imperfections. He was pursuing me long before I knew I needed to be pursued. I felt I was all His, not knowing that this was something I would have to learn, and keep on learning for a long time to come! It took a lot of shaking to wake me up.

Several years later, after I had made my perpetual profession of vows, the crisis came. A series of circumstances knocked the bottom out of my life. After months of anguish, confusion, hurt, and loneliness, I had nowhere to turn but to the Lord. I suddenly realized that I had indeed been "squandering my heritage in a far country" by being so preoccupied with myself, my reputation, etc. With freedom and joy, I realized that my Father did not mind being a last resort, and that He was waiting for me with open arms and a wide-open heart.

It was only then that my heart was awakened, and I began to learn the meaning of prayer. This was the first time I asked the Lord what *He* wanted of me, and only then did I make my real commitment to Him, choosing to remain forever in the service of my Master, and begging Him to open my ears, that His Word might truly be my life.

As my friend learned, God wants us. He meets us. He takes us forward. He wants us to be holy. The apostle Paul wrote to the Christians in Corinth: "So, if you think you are standing firm, be careful that you don't fall! No temptation has seized you except what is common to man. And God is faithful; he will not let you be tempted beyond what you can bear. But when you are tempted, he will also provide a way out so that you can stand up under it" (1 Corinthians 10:12-13, NIV). He chose us before we chose Him. He wants to bring us safely home, through every temptation.

❧

His Power to Transform

Jesus doesn't start from nothing as He conforms us to His

own likeness. It is a divine principle that His saving and transforming power act upon the stuff we are made of, our personalities, our tastes, our prejudices, our experiences. If we present ourselves to Him to be made over into His likeness, the holy version will bear a relationship to what we were before we came to Him.

After all, He created everything in the first place. It's all His and He can transform it easily. He's the one who changed water into wine. He's the one who multiplied two fish and five loaves into enough food for more than five thousand people. He used dirt and His own spit, the materials He had at hand, to make a poultice for the blind man's eyes. Each of the transformed creations were fabricated from something He had created in the first place.

By the same principle, we know that He does not disregard the kind of person we are when He calls us. Are you by nature impatient? He can transform your impatience into a holy boldness. (Think of Peter.) Are you timid? He can transform your fearfulness into a complete reliance on His strength. (Think of Timothy.) Are you an ordinary, unnoticed housewife? He can make you a Christ-bearer. (Think of Mary.)

The Lord is ready to make strong servants out of the worst of us. But we must believe it; we must come to Him in faith for forgiveness and deliverance and then go out to do the work He has given us to do.

Trust and Obey

There is in each one of us a kind of homelessness, a deep, unspoken, inexpressible longing for a safe place away from the clamor. Without God, most of the world tries to satisfy that longing with more money, more leisure, more things. Christians know that is futile, and yet we too hold back from choosing to cling to Him with single-hearted determination.

It is pride, the root of all sins, that often holds us back. We imagine we can handle things quite well on our own, or we fear that God is likely to tell us to do something we don't want to do. The whole Christian life is a process of bringing the self-life down to death in order that the life of Jesus may be manifest in us. "As he grows greater, I must grow less," said John the Baptist (John 3:30). Holiness presupposes constant growth through an ongoing relationship with the One who has called us to be holy.

Our pride sometimes causes us to make unnecessary crosses for ourselves:

Let us remember that it is not God who makes many of the crosses that we find in our way, such as we commonly call "crosses." Our Heavenly Father makes "straight paths for our feet,"... But when the path that God points out goes north and south, and our stubborn wills lead us east and west, the consequence is *"a cross"*—a cross of our own making, not that which our Master bids us "take up and carry after Him," and of which our Master bids us "take up and carry after Him," and of which it has been well said, "He always carries the heaviest end Himself."*

Even in this complicated century, the path to holiness remains the same as it was in the first century after Jesus was born:

- *prayer and meditation* (quiet time apart with God, listening to Him, thinking about what He tells us, learning to trust Him), followed by
- *simple obedience* to what He has said.

Prayer and Meditation
Regardless of how many times in a week we may attend church or read our Bibles, personal prayer is absolutely vital to our growth in trust and holiness. We need it every

*Annie Webb-Peploe, quoted by Mary Tileston in *Joy and Strength* (Minneapolis: World Wide Publications, 1986), 354.

day, ideally in the early morning when we are least likely to be interrupted. Prayer enables our hearts to be established in a place of peace that can carry us through anything the day may bring. Jesus Himself, who was busier and more in demand than any of us, got up "a great while before day" to commune with His Father. He knew that without prayer, He could not carry on for the next fifteen hours.

When I start to pray, I just put myself in God's presence. Psalm 46 urges us to "be still and know that I am God." I don't talk much. In essence, I say to Him, "Lord, here I am. I want to hear You. I'm ready to be shown." It is as difficult for me to generate "spiritual" feelings as it is for anybody else. I don't wait for them. (Often, however, I prime the pump a bit by singing a hymn or reading from my Bible.) Like almost everyone else, I tend to feel scattered and restless. I think of things I need to remember to do during the day. An easy solution to that problem is to have a pencil and paper with which to write down the things I remember. Then I don't have to keep reminding myself about them and they'll wait for my attention later.

Most of us start our times of prayer with a rendition of our worries and requests. We *can* resist that tendency and quiet our overactive minds before Him. He knows everything. There is enough time. I keep a prayer list, the people I want to remember to pray for and the concerns about which I am not yet at peace. I try to pray for whatever is on the list unhurriedly instead of fretfully.

Sometimes we need the help of written prayers. I grew up in a family and a church where we were very suspicious of anybody reading a prayer. We thought that if it was not spontaneous, God was not going to listen to it. Some time later, I realized that the Bible itself is full of written prayers, including the one Jesus taught His disciples when they asked for a model of prayer. "Our Father who art in heaven ..." (Matthew 6:9-13). The older I get, the more I use that prayer and the more I realize that virtually everything that really matters is contained in that one prayer. I am not praying to get an answer to every question or a solution to every problem, but rather to put my whole life and all the lives of those whom I love in the light of heaven.

If quiet prayer is the foundation of my long day, the first place I go after I wake up, the first conversation in which I engage, it is going to make a difference in everything I do later. Beginning the day with prayer instills a joyful calmness in me that I can bring to the people I encounter throughout the day.

Simple Obedience

After I have consulted Him directly and through His Word and He has reminded me of what I must do, I obey. There are only two choices. The rule of heaven is "Thy will be done." The rule of hell is "*My* will be done." If I'm praying, "Thy will be done," then presumably I'm prepared to cooperate with it.

Sometimes we get grandiose ideas for schemes we'd love to accomplish for God. Once in a great while, they are truly God's will. Most of the time, however, His will for us is to do the humble and down-to-earth thing, something for which nobody will ever thank us.

Holy people are always down-to-earth folks. As we learn to trust and obey, we can ask Him to send us people to imitate. God will answer such prayers. When I went to Bible College in Alberta, Canada, far away from my childhood home in New Jersey, God provided an example of holiness for me in the form of a radiant older woman I called Mom Cunningham. She had pink cheeks, twinkly eyes, a perpetual smile, and a lovely Scottish accent. Over tea and scones, I would pour out my heart and she would listen. I don't remember much of what she said, except that she almost always quoted to me Romans 15:13: "May the God of hope fill you with all joy and peace in believing." She must have noticed that the lonely girl across the table seemed to need more joy and peace in believing. She modeled it for me as she loved me and brought my needs to the Father in prayer.

Mom Cunningham protected me from copying a pretentious holiness as she told me about her failures. She was honest about her relationship with God. After her husband died, she told me about her many regrets, the things she should have done and the things she shouldn't have done. She prayed, "Lord, why didn't you help me? Why didn't you show me?" She said He responded with deep love, "Because you weren't ready to be shown."

As you and I pursue the way of holiness, may each one of us be "ready to be shown."

🌿 Six 🌿

*W*alking With Jesus

What a relief—after we have turned our lives over to our Savior Jesus, we do not need to be in charge of them any longer. The One whose invitation we have responded to loves us with absolute affection and wisdom, and He shoulders full responsibility for our welfare thereafter. It is entirely possible for us to wander off the path, and yet as we return to Him and go on through our days and years with Him, we learn just how trustworthy He is. Walking alongside such a Savior proves to be a life of happy surprises, one full of intriguing twists on our otherwise comparatively improvised version of life. Our love and our obedience walk hand in hand. "If anyone obeys his word, God's love is truly made complete in him. This is how we know we are in him: Whoever claims to live in him must walk as Jesus did" (1 John 2:5-6, NIV).

Walking with Jesus does not imply "obedience or else." We are under new auspices, for which we are everlastingly grateful. It is altogether possible to practice a form of obedience to a tyrant or to a neutral authority such as the traffic police out of respect or fear of consequences, and yet it is only possible for us to practice *wholehearted* obedience to someone if we enjoy an intimate relationship with him or her. What a joy it is to obey this Lord, who provides us with His Spirit to counsel and empower us and who ensures that everything that happens to us, even the cyclone that brings nothing but destruction, has come through the hedge of His love before it reaches us.

Apparently, from the Lord's point of view, our trusting obedience is one of the most important things in the universe. Jesus tells us, "Not everyone who says to me, 'Lord, Lord,' will enter the kingdom of heaven, but only he who does the will of my Father who is in heaven" (Matthew 7:21, NIV). Maintaining our effort to learn to obey His will becomes all-important.

People object, saying, "I simply do not know what to *do!* The Bible is confusing. I wish it covered every detail." Yes, but He did that on purpose. *Not* knowing His will in every circumstance heightens our awareness of our need for Him and enhances our ongoing relationship with Him. The Bible is not a rule book. We do find lots of rules in it, but they are not clustered together in one place and they do not cover every exigency. Jesus did not give us a one-size-fits-all formula. To a literalist, He will always prove to be the most elusive of teachers. In fact, there is very little of the letter of the law in what He tells us. A rule-bound system simply cannot keep up with His darting illumination. Had He meant for us to follow a prescription for every behavior, no relationship would have been necessary beyond the relationship with the pages of a book. The Law, says the writer of the letter to the Hebrews, is incapable of bringing anybody to maturity. Rules, codes, and policies are deadening. They cannot stimulate growth. No organizational policy, no set of tacit assumptions from your culture or religious group, will lead you to the full freedom of mature character that your sonship will do—characterized by independent, freely-given obedience.

Yes, it's difficult to reconcile what seem to be some glaring contradictions. Should you hate "even the garment spotted by the flesh," as Jude advises, and "avoid such people" as Timothy tells us, or should you "bear all things" in love as Paul counseled the Corinthians? Those seeming inconsistencies simply provide us with more opportunities to get down on our knees and ask Him, "Lord, how am I supposed to apply this right now? Lord, show me what to do." The Lord loves to hear prayers like that. He will hear you and He will help you. Do you think the Shepherd is going to make it hard for the sheep to follow Him? The Shepherd is much more interested in making sure that the sheep get to where they belong than the sheep are in getting there—much more interested. I wish I had understood that when I was in high school and college, when I was so worried about missing the will of God.

The same God who urges us to obey also furnishes the desire as well as the strength to do so. Our part is to exercise our wills. This is far from quietism or pietism, in which a person is completely passive and expects God to do everything. Walking with Jesus means that His grace is at work in my human nature, making me willing to be taught, willing to be shown, and willing to do whatever He tells me:

> *If anyone loves me, he will obey my teaching. My Father will love him, and we will come to him and make our home with him. He who does not love me will not obey my teaching. These words you hear are not my own; they belong to the Father who sent me.... The Counselor, the Holy Spirit, whom the Father will send in my name, will teach you all things and will remind you of everything I have said to you. Peace I leave with you; my peace I give you. I do not give to you as the world gives. Do not let your hearts be troubled and do not be afraid.*
>
> JOHN 14:23-24, 26-27, NIV

Although God has deliberately left us in a quandary about many things, think of the crop of dwarfs He would have reared if He had made it all black and white. He did not leave us with a rule book; He left us with His own living Spirit. He wants us to reach maturity. He is not interested in conformity to a static code but to a Person, the living expression of Himself, the "likeness of His Son."

Paul stated it even more comprehensively, "to know him." To know Christ is to be made like Him. Paul's fellow worker, Epaphras, shared his vision: "He prays constantly and earnestly for you, that you may become mature Christians, and may fulfill God's will for you" (Colossians 4:12, PHILLIPS).

The Simplicity of Obedience

When you walk with Jesus, you plant your feet on the same three steps at the beginning of every enterprise:

1. You present your body as a "living sacrifice." Say to the Lord, "I need Your guidance and help. I'll do anything You tell me." You make that commitment *before* you know what He is going to tell you.

Remember the link between presenting yourself as a living sacrifice (Romans 12:1) and obedience. Even if all you are bringing Him is your perplexity or your broken heart, He will receive it. "The sacrifice acceptable to God is a broken spirit, a broken and contrite heart, O God, you will not despise" (Psalm 51:17, NRSV). The giving of yourself to Him demonstrates your trust, your thanksgiving, and your "spiritual worship." It makes a statement about who God is.

2. *You pray and read your Bible.* You cannot obtain His guidance and help if you don't arrange time to be with God alone. Remember that you are not reading a rule book. Even the Ten Commandments, written on stone tablets, were not the last word. They needed to be interpreted and applied to specific situations. "Thou shalt not kill"— except in certain conditions, such as when God commands you to wipe out an enemy. The voice of God's Spirit gives specific instructions for your "instant" or specific situation.

3. *You do what you know.* Do the thing you are sure that God wants you to do today. It wastes energy to direct your attention past the simple duties of today and start worrying about tomorrow. Do you have a huge decision that you are worried about? Leave it in God's hands and go about your ordinary duties, trusting that as you are faithful in doing the work He has given you today, your decision will be perfectly clear when the time comes. Leave the littlest matters in His hands as well.

Over and over in the small matters of daily life, I have been nudged to trust Him. Carelessly, I may have lost a favorite pen. When I discover that it's missing, I want to stop all my work, turn everything upside down and empty every wastebasket in the house to search for an item that, strictly speaking, I don't need right now because I have my computer running and I am not writing anything by hand. The Lord reminds me, "Forget about the lost pen. Finish the job you are doing right now." Amazingly, when I finish my task at the computer, the Lord brings to my mind the one place I wouldn't have looked on my own, and the lost pen is found.

Obedience School

As we learn to proceed trustingly through the petty matters of our daily lives, obedience in the big things becomes instinctive and the cultivation of an obedient attentiveness to the Master becomes a way of life. In due time, we can be counted among the "mature, who by constant use have trained themselves to distinguish good from evil" (Hebrews 5:14, NIV). God calls us sons. A son is far different from a servant. A servant has very little liberty to exercise his own preferences. He is employed for a specific task and he is told exactly how and when to perform it. A son is not trained for a job, but for a life.

Obedience to God comes to us more instinctively if we have been blessed with parents and loving caretakers who could set us on that path early in life. My parents were honest and orderly and they expected their six children to grow to be the same way. They believed that a child should be asked to do something one time only. Failure to respond was the equivalent of disobedience. My mother used a hairbrush to spank us sometimes, but most of the time she used a flexible switch. Because she started disciplining us when we were very young, she hardly ever had to use the switch on most of us; her firm words were enough. However, we have stories about my brother Dave, who was the most mischievous child in the family. One time, Mother put him in his room to sit in a chair for a certain length of time, and when the time was up, she returned to check on him. The door was still closed and she had not heard anybody leave the room, but Dave was nowhere to be found. Lo and behold, he was sitting on the appointed chair, but he had moved the chair to the porch roof, which was under the window of his room. Another time, she told Dave, "If you don't straighten up, I have my stick handy, and I'm going to use it." Dave's response: "I've got my legs handy, and I'm going to use them!"

Over the years, because of my speaking engagements, my husband and I have been invited to a good many church suppers. It has been an eye-opening experience, to say the least, as we have been subjected to the spectacle of "kids first"—rushing the buffet table like gangbusters, cleaning up the desserts and potato chips, rollicking wildly around the church basement making a din while the grown-ups shrug and say, "Kids will be kids, you know."

We do know of a large church in New Jersey with a lot of families of remarkably well-behaved children. They do not provide children's church and the children sit with their parents throughout the service, which includes a one-hour sermon. No climbing over the backs of the pews or running down the aisles to the bathroom or scribbling on the bulletin. It is a testimony to early discipline. The result? Peace for everyone, including the children.

Benefits of Obedience

Peace is only one of the benefits of walking obediently with Jesus. In broader terms, the best reward of obedience is the privilege of living in company with God. Obedient love establishes and maintains an unshakable unity. We mere mortals are able to *know* Him.

Obedience also makes us able to walk without fear. When Paul was sailing as a prisoner to Italy and was about to be wrecked in the Mediterranean Sea, everyone on board was terror-stricken. The soldiers and captain were sure they were doomed and some tried to escape overboard. But Paul, in obedience to God's message through an angel, encouraged them to eat some bread and stay with the ship. All were saved.

Obedience can assuage grief. My Great-Aunt Alice served as a hostess in a rest house in Virginia during World War I. She had never before worked for a living, but after her husband one day dropped dead at the bank where he worked, she had to find a way to support herself. So she opened her home to soldiers and sailors, many of whom were terribly homesick, some of them just back from the front with permanent disabilities. Her own grief and her uncertainties about the future were made manageable by plunging into a round of duties for the sake of others.

Ezekiel the prophet responded obediently to the loss of his beloved wife:

> *"Son of man, with one blow I am about to take away from you the delight of your eyes. Yet do not lament or weep or shed any tears. Groan quietly; do not mourn for the dead. Keep your turban fastened and your sandals on your feet; do not cover the lower part of your face or eat the customary food of mourners."... In the evening my wife died. The next morning I did as I had been commanded.*
>
> EZEKIEL 24:16-18, NIV

For the sake of conveying an important prophetic message to the people, God asked of Ezekiel more than any human being would dare to ask, but He knew His man.

Ezekiel had had plenty of practice in obedience, and it was not his habit to bridle. His obedient submission helped him handle the enormity of his loss.

Our obedience may lead us not to the fulfillment of our ideals but to very unexpected and "unspiritual" situations. I may have been wondering which house to buy or what job to take and my simple prayer, the often glibly pronounced "Thy will be done," may carry me far into regions I never meant to approach in the land of Humility and Sanctification. Nobody gets close to God except those who have been sanctified. All that it takes to bring me home to God is at one and the same time a part of the process of making me fit to live with Him.

Jesus' Obedience

We are told that Jesus Himself had to learn obedience through what He suffered (Hebrews 5:8). During Jesus' three years as an itinerant rabbi He knew what it was to be weary, hungry, and homeless. The common people heard Him gladly but the religious elite could not stand Him. He was misquoted, misjudged, misrepresented, misunderstood. The Hebrew scholars were forever laying traps for Him, challenging, quarreling, quibbling. He was praised and scorned, followed and forsaken, loved and hated, listened to and rejected, crowned and crucified. He had every reason to feel lonely in the world of men, but it was thus that He "learned" and demonstrated for us the meaning of obedience—through the things that He suffered.

Before the start of His brief public ministry, He whose hands had made the worlds learned obedience in a dusty carpenter shop. When Joseph showed Him how to use a tool, did he hold the little hands in his and say, "Like this. Hold it this way"? The boy had to *learn*. He did not make tables and benches by divine fiat. He made them with tools held in human hands. He had to *learn* the skills, learn to be thorough, dependable, prompt, faithful. If He was ever tempted to cut corners, He did not yield to the temptation. He did nothing sloppily. He worked carefully, thoroughly, dependably, promptly, faithfully. Surely He was gracious with the customers. He *grew* "in favor with God and man" (Luke 2:52, NKJV). The cheerful acceptance of humble work, the small testings of any boy's home life were a part of His preparation for the great testings of His public years, a part of the road which led Him to the cross.

To walk with Him is to walk the Way of the Cross. If the cross we are asked to take up is not presented to us in the form of martyrdom, heroic action of some kind, dragons or labyrinths or even "ministry"—at least something that looks spiritual—are we to conclude that we have missed the Way? Not at all. Sometimes the humblest life, such as that of "Mom" Cunningham (mentioned in chapter 5) is the clearest example of obedience. The Way of the Cross is an ordinary street in an ordinary city. It is an ordinary life lived in the grace of God. There is a pot of gold, there is a king's reward, but it comes at the end of the journey.

Heaven in Our Hands

Obedience to what we know of God's will opens the way for more blessings than we knew existed. We find joy along a journey that at times can be taxing. Walking with Jesus proves to be, at the least, not boring.

Remember Abraham's servant, who was dispatched to find a hometown wife for Isaac. His assignment must have seemed like a tall order. Without so much as the brush of an angel's wing to direct him, he found the right town and decided to wait for the young women to come to draw water at the public well. Using an inventive way of ascertaining divine favor, he asked God to let the virgin who was right for his master's son be identified by her generous willingness to serve him. His method worked. Rebekah responded instantly to his request for a drink, and then took initiative on her own to water his ten camels. "Blessed be the Lord, the God of my master Abraham," he said. "As for me, being on the way, the Lord led me" (Genesis 24:27, KJV).

That is how it is when we're walking with Him. "Being on the way," walking in loving relationship with our Savior, our feet are directed onto the right path every time. We go the distance with Him, all the way to heaven.

As you therefore have received Christ Jesus the Lord, so walk in Him, having been firmly rooted and now being built up in Him and established in your faith, just as you were instructed, and overflowing with gratitude.

COLOSSIANS 2:6, NASB

Seven

A Servant Heart

The idea of leadership is very popular in Christian circles these days. People write books about leadership, Christian magazines feature articles about leadership, and flyers advertise special courses or conferences.

Sometimes I get invited to speak about leadership, but, truth be told, I am not very eager to talk about it. Usually, I warn the people who've asked me that yes, I can speak on that topic; however, my emphasis will be on *servanthood*, not on "effective" or "powerful" leadership. I tell them that because our Lord and Master Jesus was the Servant of all, I believe that a leader must be a servant first and always.

In Jesus' day, the Pharisees found this difficult to understand. They were men who appreciated public recognition and the exercise of power. They noticed that crowds of people were following this obscure rabbi and that His authority held much sway over the people. They became jealous of His popularity and influence. Little did they know that one of His leadership-training techniques was, of all things, *foot-washing*.

We know the story: Jesus the Teacher and Healer, took

the position of the household servant who was lowest of all, stripped off His outer garments and wrapped a towel around His waist. Carrying a basin of water, He carefully washed the feet of each disciple, even Judas, whom He knew would soon betray Him into the hands of crucifiers, and Peter, whom He knew would later deny being His disciple.

> *When he had finished washing their feet, he put on his clothes and returned to his place. "Do you understand what I have done for you?" he asked them. "You call me 'Teacher' and 'Lord,' and rightly so, for that is what I am. Now that I, your Lord and Teacher, have washed your feet, you also should wash one another's feet. I have set you an example that you should do as I have done for you. I tell you the truth, no servant is greater than his master, nor is a messenger greater than the one who sent him. Now that you know these things, you will be blessed if you do them."*
>
> JOHN 13:12-17, NIV

This is almost as difficult for us to grasp as it was for the Pharisees. The apostle Paul said that he was willing "to spend and to be spent for you" (2 Corinthians 12:15, KJV). Are we willing to do the same, to lay down our preferences, to sell all in order to buy the pearl of great price? Jesus said that if we are not prepared to get rid of all our possessions, we cannot be His disciples. He asks us (no exemptions for Americans) to sell all, to give up the right to ourselves, to forsake father, mother, family, possessions, home, and everything that we have, in order to be His disciples.

What does this look like?

Self-Denial

As His servants, we lay down our desire for a certain quality of life, our insistence that our life must be arranged in a certain way in order to be acceptable. In a word, we deny ourselves. Making a radical departure from the ways of the world around us, we accept the fact that our preferences and our agendas will not be honored. After all, what are we but mere bondservants who have been bought with a price? As His servants, we pay attention to how we react to slights and hurts, because we realize that wherever we are being self-protective or irritated, we most likely do not yet possess a servant's heart.

We also accept (with joy, because it represents a great spiritual liberation), the menial tasks that come our way, knowing that God is more interested in our response than He is in the tangible results. One day I noticed the footnote to Romans 12:16 in my NIV Bible: "'Live in harmony with one another. Do not be proud, but be willing to associate with people of low position.' Note: 'Be willing to do menial work.'" As servants, we are willing to do menial work; we don't grouse about it. Christians are not TGIF (Thank God It's Friday) people nor are they Blue Monday people.

When I lived with the Auca Indians for two years, I learned more about servanthood than I had known from my Christian upbringing. The Auca men left the clearing every morning by six o'clock if it wasn't absolutely pouring rain, and they didn't return to the settlement until five or six o'clock in the late afternoon, having run or walked barefoot thirty miles or so looking for food. The women would go out to the fields as soon as they had taken care of the babies and fed the small children and had eaten whatever might be left over for them. At the end of the day, an Auca woman would come home carrying her fifty- or sixty-pound basket of manioc and plantains by a strap over her forehead, usually with a baby on her hip and a machete in the other hand, caked with sweat and mud from head to toe. She would walk into her house, stoop down to drop the basket behind her, and set to work stirring up the fire, cooking the food, very calmly and quietly doing the things that needed to be done before the family went to bed.

Sometimes far-away Westerners, who had little idea of

the actual situation, commended me for my "wonderful work," probably because they thought of it as difficult, isolated, dangerous, or even nobly sacrificial. There were others who for the very same reason condemned me, for I had had the audacity to take my three-year-old into that setting. Some envied me, some pitied me, some admired, some criticized. I could not help but ask myself if perhaps I had been mistaken to come. Was I really obeying God, or had I merely obeyed some misguided impulse, some lust for distinction, some masochistic urge to bury myself in that forsaken place? I became reconciled to my situation by watching the Indians, serving each other and me untroubled by the relative value of their work, free of the pressures of competition or comparison. There was for me here a lesson in simplicity and acceptance of one's place in life, which, because I was a Christian, I could take from the hand of God. My duty was one thing, theirs another. My responsibility lay there for the time being. The responsibility of some of my correspondents who gazed starry-eyed at my role lay perhaps in an office or a kitchen or the cockpit of an airplane.

Self-Effacement

When I get to heaven, I want to hear the words, "Well done, good and faithful *servant*," not "good job, excellent and committed CEO." In spite of the clamor of society around us, the urgings to succeed and conquer, I would rather emulate my fellow believers who have taken the narrow, lower way.

One of them, a seventeenth-century monk, has influenced generations of Christians through a slender volume called *The Practice of the Presence of God*. Born Nicholas Herman in French Lorraine, he became a Lay brother with the Discalced (barefoot) Carmelites in Paris in 1666 and was known thereafter as "Brother Lawrence." He was undistinguished in academic matters and ended up in the kitchen of the monastery, where he found that the most menial tasks could bring him nearer to heaven. He died when he was eighty years old, having become a bit of a legend in his own time for his cheerful servant's heart, his love, and his willingness to choose the humble path.

If we ever get the idea that any job is beneath us, we're off the path of Jesus. My second husband, Addison Leitch, was the dean of a college. One evening he was told that pranksters had slathered peanut butter and shaving cream all over the walls of a certain men's dormitory. So he made his way over there and went down the halls knocking on doors, asking if anybody knew how the mess had gotten there. Nobody had a clue. "I had a couple of choices," he said. "We had a wonderful janitor who would do anything for anybody, anytime. But I didn't want to take advantage of that man at that hour of the night. I could either force the students to come out and clean it up themselves or I could call the janitor, which I had decided I wasn't going to do. So I decided to do something different. I went and got a bucket and a brush, and started scrubbing the walls myself." It wasn't very long before heads began to pop out of the doors one by one and the guys saw their dean scrubbing down the walls. One after another, they located rags and began to help him. What a simple example of servanthood.

My own dormitory experience also helped me understand servanthood. My housemother at Wheaton College had come from a very wealthy home in Augusta, Georgia, one with "white columns in the front and many servants in the back." Her family had disinherited her after she became a Christian. Like most Southern belles, she had been raised to be beautiful and to be a "lady." There she was, single and with a good classical education but no particular skills. She certainly had never expected to have to make a living for herself.

Somehow, she made her way to Wheaton, and she and I became friends. In her wonderful Georgia accent, she called me "Baaeeddy" (Betty), stringing the "e" into two or three syllables as only someone from Georgia can do. We used to walk to Sunday school together because she was my teacher.

One day she said to me (charmingly clasping her very

ample bosom), "Oh, Baaeeddy, I came to Wheaton to be a spiritual counselor, but here I am carrying mops and toilet paper across the campus." She was a spiritual counselor, of course, to me and to several hundred other girls. And the very fact that she was willing to carry the mops and toilet paper tremendously enhanced the effectiveness of her message as a spiritual counselor.

Years later, when she was living in a retirement home in Florida, my second husband, Add Leitch, and I visited her. Now somewhat smaller and gray-haired, she still had the wonderful smile. I reminded her of what it had meant to me for her to be willing to carry mops and toilet paper across the campus. Again in her charming accent, she exclaimed, "Oh, Baaeeddy! Just think of the mercy of God, that He allowed me to carry mops and toilet paper for His glory!"

Cooperation With God

There is no better example of servanthood than motherhood, because mothers are literally cooperating with God in His creative work of bringing another human being into this world. He needs a mother's body in order to do that; He doesn't create people in any other way. He requires the cooperation of one woman and one man to bring that child into being.

Cooperation with God entails self-effacement, self-denial, and all the rest. I have had the opportunity to speak at many women's weekend retreats, where the hostesses go to tremendous effort to make everything perfect. In many of those places, it takes quite a chunk of time at the end to thank all those who have served. Sometimes I have wondered how many volunteers they might have gotten if the women were told in advance that there would not be any public recognition of their service.

I am reminded often of the humble heart and willing hands of Mrs. Kershaw, the elderly woman hired by my mother to "do for" our large family. The first time I ever saw her, I had come home from college for Christmas vacation. In her letters to me, Mother had been writing about this lovely lady who was now working for her. I walked into the kitchen, and here was this very hump-backed lady bent over the dishpan with her back to me. I exclaimed, "Oh, this must be Mrs. Kershaw, isn't it!" She didn't move a muscle. My sister was standing on the other side of the kitchen, and she said, "She's deaf."

I said, "You mean, she can't hear you at all?"

"No!"

"Not even if you shout?"

And Ginny shouted, "Not even if you shout!"

Still Mrs. Kershaw didn't flinch, so I went over and tapped her on the shoulder, and she turned around, a radiant smile lighting up her face. "Oh, here's the daughter!" (She always called me "the daughter." My sister was "Ginny," but I was "the daughter.")

One day I came across a list of the things she had done during a typical day. My mother apparently had planned to go out for the day and had made a list of duties for Mrs. Kershaw, careful as usual not to overload her. Mrs. Kershaw had made her own counterpart list to report back to my mother. Between "Did dishes" and "Did ironing," she had written "Rested, and had prayer for all." This was repeated more than one time. "Swept floor," "Made applesauce," and "Rested, and had prayer for all." And, somewhere in the middle, "Visited with Nana."

One of the daily tasks that was uppermost in Mother's mind was to keep her stepmother, who was confined to her room upstairs, company. We children were very remiss in the way we treated our stepgrandmother, because she was a very gloomy person to be around. We didn't like to go into her room.

Mother would encourage us to go visit her. "Please go in and talk to Nana." We would always say, "What in the world are we supposed to talk about? She is not interested in anything." But Mrs. Kershaw would go upstairs willingly to talk to her, whether it appeared on her list or not. Their conversations were worth overhearing, because not only was Mrs. Kershaw totally deaf, so was Nana. Whatever Mrs. Kershaw would say had nothing to do with what Nana would say. My grandmother hardly smiled at all, but Mrs. Kershaw never stopped smiling, bringing sunshine wherever she went, "resting and praying" for our whole family.

At His Service

Besides self-denial, self-effacement, and a willingness to cooperate with God, a true servant puts his or her gifts at the disposal of the Master. We tend to assume that God wants to use our highest-ranked gifts, but that may not be the case.

Once a former missionary came to me with a grievance. She had come back from the mission field to her home church and had told her pastor that she was available to serve in any way that she could. "Elisabeth, he asked me to take charge of the nursery! I explained to him that I have three degrees and that in all my fifteen years on the mission field I had not taken care of babies. I have other experience: teaching Bible classes, organizing a school. And he insisted that what he really needed was a nursery worker! I told him that I did not feel I could do that."

"What did he say?" I asked.

"Well, then he asked me to bake bread for communion. I don't think he understood my qualifications."

This lady was asking the wrong person for advice. I said, "I think you should go back to him and tell him that you'll

take charge of the nursery and you'll bake the bread, too."
She was quite hurt.

I wonder how Jesus compares that attitude with, for
instance, the attitude of Amy Carmichael, who would not
ask anybody to take on a job that she herself was not
willing to do. When there was a cholera epidemic in the
village of Dohnavur, Amy gathered up her pail of disinfec-
tant and her rags and went down into the little village huts
where nobody else would go, not even the doctors. She
scrubbed and she saved lives. "Verily, verily, I say unto
you, the servant is not greater than his lord; neither he that
is sent greater than he that sent him. If ye know these
things, happy are ye if ye do them" (John 13:16-17, KJV).
There is great happiness in having a servant's heart.

This was the same woman who had had a very effective
ministry as an itinerant evangelist for the first seven or
eight years she was in India. She had a small band of godly
Indian women who traveled with her by bullock cart,
bumping along rutted roads from one remote village to
another, reaching out to Hindu women who were
sequestered in the inner courts of their homes. In the
opinion of the Indians as well as Amy's European sup-
porters, this was true "spiritual work."

Then came the day when a little girl appeared on her
veranda as she was having her morning tea, having
escaped (only God knows how) from the captivity of being

a child prostitute in the Hindu temple. Appalled at the practices of the temples and the conditions under which small children were raised, Amy began to take them into her own compound. This meant, according to the Indian Tamil proverb which says, "children tie the mother's feet," that Amy could no longer be an itinerant evangelist. Her gifts were "on the shelf" and she found herself doing the last thing she would have imagined when she came to India, mixing formula and changing diapers and finding workers to help her. She once said, "I must have cut tens of thousands of tiny toenails and fingernails!"

And inasmuch as Amy did it to one of the least of those babies, she did it for Jesus Himself. ("Inasmuch as ye have done it unto one of the least of these my brethren, ye have done it unto me," Matthew 25:40.) Some of the women who had been part of the itinerant evangelistic band had come from high-caste Indian homes, and the daily duties of orphanage work were anathema to them. The spiritual work of traveling from village to village was one thing, but changing diapers and wiping little runny noses was quite another. (Even into the 1980s, 98 percent of the nurses in India were Christians, because Hindus would not do that kind of work.) So Amy, who had been raised in a very wealthy home in Ireland, showed them what servanthood is like and gradually taught them how "the servant is not greater than his master" (John 13:16). In part because of her willingness to lay down her gifts, she became a true leader, and to this day we see the fruits of her ministry for the kingdom of God.

It's a tall order to take the lowest place, to lay it all at His feet, and to listen for His next small wish. Yoked with Him, we can do this as easily as we can conquer more exalted worlds.

❧ Eight ❧

ℋelps in Prayer

L et my prayer be counted as incense before thee" (Psalm 141:2, RSV).

"The four living creatures and the twenty-four elders fell down before the Lamb, each holding a harp, and with golden bowls full of incense, which are the prayers of the saints" (Revelation 5:8, RSV).

In these verses, our prayers are described as being "like incense" to God. *All* of our prayers are included, from the most eloquent ones to the most inarticulate groanings. What is incense good for? It appears to serve no practical purpose at all, and its smoke and fragrance soon dissipate. Our prayers are like that because they seem to accomplish little and they soon vanish, but God likes the smell of them.

Jesus prayed: He offered thanksgiving, He interceded for others, He made petitions. That the Son—coequal, coeternal, consubstantial with the Father—should need to come to the Father in prayer is a mystery. That we, God's children, should be not only permitted but commanded to come is a mystery also. How does prayer work? Can we change the mind of a sovereign and omnipotent God? Does it matter when and how we utter our prayers?

We do not understand. We simply pray because this is how spiritual things have been set up. Just as the physical law of gravity causes the book to fall to the floor if I drop it, spiritual power is released through prayer. Generations of believers can testify that God meets us in prayer. He meets us because we invite Him to be with us, believing like children that our Father loves us. Our praying is not some kind of internal dialogue or an exercise in futility. God is listening.

Prayer Closets

Christians may pray anytime and anywhere, but we cannot well do without a special time and place to be alone with God each day. Although we are often advised to pray very early in the morning, most of us find that early morning is not an easy time to pray. I wonder if there is an *easy* time. The simple fact is that early morning is probably the *only* time when we can be fairly sure of not being interrupted, unless we are mothers of small children.

Where can we pray? The Lord advised us to go into our "closet" (Matthew 6:6), meaning any place apart from the eyes and the ears of others. Jesus went to the hills, to the wilderness, to a garden; His disciples to the seashore or to an upper room; Peter to a housetop. We may need to find a literal closet or a bathroom or a parked car. We may take a walk outdoors and pray. We may be confined to a wheel-chair or a bed. But every day we must *arrange* a time and place to be alone with God, to talk to Him and to listen to Him.

When I stumble out of bed in the morning, put on a robe, and go into my study, words do not spring sponta-neously to my lips, except perhaps, "Lord, here I am again to talk to you. It's cold. I'm not feeling very spiritual...." To help myself pray, I try to place myself consciously in the presence of God. Sometimes, I might look out my window to catch a glimpse of God's creation. Everything out there is worshiping Him, every tree, every insect, the sky itself. All of heaven is worshiping as well, every hour of the day and night. Imagine! Here I am, a solitary individual, joining with the cherubim, seraphim, angels, archangels, and all of creation in praising our Creator and Sustainer.

Even with this in mind, praying is rarely easy for me. The apostle Paul said we "wrestle" in prayer, and that "our fight is not against any physical enemy; it is against organizations and powers that are spiritual. We are up against the unseen powers that control this dark world, and spiritual agents from the very headquarters of evil" (Ephesians 6:12, PHILLIPS). Seldom do we consider the nature of our opponent, and that is to his advantage. When we do recognize him for what he is, however, we have an inkling as to why prayer is so difficult. It's the weapon that

Unseen Power dreads most, and if he can get us to treat it casually, he can keep his hold.

As I grow old, I find that I am more conscious than ever of my need to pray, but at the same time it seems to become more of a struggle. It is harder to concentrate, for one thing. I seem to run short of words. Sometimes I feel the pressure of my undone tasks; there is so much to do. In an emergency, my words burst forth: "Oh, God!" "Lord, help me!" During my ordinary quiet times, however, I tend to lapse into silence or to run through my prayer lists mechanically. It helps me to remember that I am here not only to pepper God with entreaties but also to *adore* Him. God is *looking* for worshipers. Will He always have to go to a church to find them, or might there be one here and there in an ordinary house, kneeling alone by a chair, simply loving Him?

When the Answer Is "No"
C.S. Lewis wrote, "Prayer is request. The essence of request, as distinct from compulsion, is that it may or may not be granted. And if an infinitely wise Being listens to the requests of finite and foolish creatures [that's you and me], of course He will sometimes grant and sometimes refuse them." When I have been confronted with an outright denial of a request I have prayed, I have tried to understand the reasons.

Why does God say "no"?

1. For the sake of other people. Jesus prayed in Geth-semane, "If it be possible, let this cup pass." God said "no" to His Son's request, for the sake of you and me. We learn from that prayer that there are some perfectly good things that are outside the will of God. Although Jim Elliot had a wife and a baby and a mission station and a whole lot of people who needed him, when I prayed for his physical safety, the answer was "no." God knew that, among other things, hundreds of people needed to be shaken up and that his wife's path needed to be radically different than what we had planned. None of it would have happened had it not been for the deaths of Jim and the other four men.

2. Because He has something better. If I pray for what looks like an egg, God is not going to give me a scorpion. However, what looks like an egg to me is often a scorpion, so God says "no." (Read Luke 11:12.) God may have something better for us, something beyond what we can imagine.

3. Because I am harboring sin. "If I had cherished sin in my heart, the Lord would not have listened" (Psalm 66:18, NIV). I may cry out to the Lord, but the heavens are like brass. He is "hiding his face" from me because of unrepented sin (see Micah 3:4). Yet, "if our hearts do not condemn us, we have confidence before God; and we receive from him whatever we ask, because we keep his commandments and do what pleases him" (1 John 3:21-22, RSV). God is faithful to help us figure out what we are doing to stymie our prayers, and He gives us the grace to step free of it.

4. *For reasons of His own that we do not need to know.* "The secret things belong to God" (Deuteronomy 29:29, RSV). Down the road, we may understand better than we do now. Gladys Aylward, a little London parlor maid with no education and no money, believed that God had called her to China as a missionary. She weighed only about eighty pounds and stood about four feet, ten inches tall. When she was growing up, black-haired Gladys had wished fervently that God would give her the same long golden hair her friends had and that she would grow to be taller, as they were. But after a long solo trek by train across Europe, Russia, and Siberia, standing on the wharf in Shanghai, she looked around and realized that God had had His own reasons for creating her just as she was. "I looked around at all the people to whom Jehovah God had sent me. Every single one of them had black hair, and every single one of them had stopped growing when I did! And I said, 'Lord God, You know what You are doing!'"

5. Because I am asking selfishly. I may not be asking for something that is in the will of God; I may be asking for the sake of my own glory. "You ask and do not receive, because you ask wrongly, to spend it on your passions" (James 4:3, RSV). Of course, God knows that we often ask amiss through ignorance. His "no" shows that He is caring for us.

"We shall come one day to a heaven where we shall gratefully know that God's great refusals were sometimes the true answers to our truest prayer," wrote P.T. Forsythe.

The Power of the Written Prayer

As I mentioned in chapter five, I grew up in a family that put the highest value on spontaneous prayers. Eventually, after struggling with wandering thoughts, my prayer vocabulary limited by the urgency of my requests, my fatigue, or my inadequate grasp of God's love, I realized that the feeling of inadequacy under which I often labored could be ameliorated by some of the "rote prayers" that I had earlier deplored. I saw that the Lord Himself had taught us one prayer that we all repeat word for word, "Our Father, who art in heaven ..." As have many others before me, I discovered that the Bible is abounding in timeless, ready-made prayers.

For example, we can use the exact words of Ephesians 1:16-19 to pray for someone:

I do not cease to give thanks for you, remembering you in my prayers, that the God of our Lord Jesus Christ, the Father of glory, may give you a spirit of wisdom and of revelation in the knowledge of him, having the eyes of your hearts enlightened, that you may know what is the hope to which he has called you, what are the riches of his glorious inheritance in the saints, and what is the immeasurable greatness of his power in us who believe, according to the working of his great might.

Nothing helps me more than the Book of Psalms. Here I find expression for my heartcries of praise, adoration, anguish, complaint, petition. It is immensely comforting to find that even David, the great king, bemoaned his loneliness; complained about his enemies and his pains, sorrows, and fears; and found ways to express praise that are far beyond my powers. I use his words and I am lifted out of myself to heights of adoration, even though I'm still the same ordinary woman alone in the same little room.

Also at the top of the list of things that have helped me in my private quiet times are the great old hymns, which express eloquently the things for which I want to pray but cannot find the words. Many hymns are prayers in themselves. I have most of them memorized, so I don't have to get a hymnbook every time I need the words. Some of my favorite prayer-hymns are "O Worship the King," "Teach Me Thy Way, O Lord," "If Thou But Suffer God to Guide Thee," "Praise, My Soul, the King of Heaven," and "The Day Thou Gavest, Lord, Is Ended."

Many people, and I am one of them, keep a prayer notebook. Families who gather to pray together sometimes maintain a family prayer notebook. My prayer notebook is not the same as my journal, which is where I record life events and truths God is showing me. For my prayer notebook, I use a little spiral notepad in which I record some of my bigger prayers with a date and a blank space after the prayer. Every now and then I go back and reread the last few pages. It is amazing and humbling to discover how many of those prayers I have forgotten—but God has answered. Of course I write His answer in the blank space, and I thank Him. (If I didn't write down the prayers, I wouldn't remember to thank Him.) It's wonderfully faith-strengthening to go back over a whole year or so to review the prayers, which at the time might have been desperate ones. The answers are always so simple. God is not worried about my life, and I can trust Him with the whole business. My notebook reminds me that my wrestling can yield to peace and refreshment, even when I remain unable to predict the answers to my prayers.

I found an anonymous prayer in my mother's little red prayer notebook, which was with her possessions after she died. She must have prayed it for me and my siblings and her grandchildren, as have I:

> Father, our children keep.
> We know not what is coming upon the earth.
> Beneath the shadow of Thy heavenly wing,
> O keep them, keep them, Thou who gavest them birth.
>
> Father, draw nearer us.
> Draw firmer around us Thy protecting arm.
> O clasp our children closer to Thy side,
> Uninjured in the day of earth's alarm.
>
> Then in Thy chambers hide,
> O hide them and preserve them calm and safe
> When sin abounds, and error flows abroad
> And Satan tempts and human passions chafe.
>
> O keep them undefiled,
> Unspotted from a tempting world of sin,
> That, clothed in white, through the bright city gates,
> They may with us in triumph enter in.

I keep a collection of such prayers, written by others, to which I resort often when my own words fall short. I prefer ancient prayers such as the *Te Deum* ("To Thee, O

God"), which was written originally in Latin. Such prayers carry me far above my own little list of concerns, circumscribed by my myopic spiritual vision.

We are just one voice in the whole collection of the heavenly creatures and all the rest of the church here on earth. There isn't a minute of any hour when the church, the body of believers all over the world, is not praying. That thought encourages me tremendously as I try to bring my own feeble prayers before God.

Ours is a walk of faith, and the One to whom we pray is absolutely capable, faithful—and He loves to smell the incense of our prayers. Whether or not we see immediate answers, we can find His peace.

Te Deum Laudamus

We praise thee, O God: we acknowledge thee to be the Lord.

All the earth doth worship thee: the Father everlasting.

To thee all Angels cry aloud: the Heavens and all the Powers therein.

To thee Cherubim and Seraphim continually do cry,

Holy, Holy, Holy, Lord God of Sabaoth;

Heaven and earth are full of the Majesty of thy Glory.

The glorious company of the Apostles praise thee.

The goodly fellowship of the Prophets praise thee.

The noble army of Martyrs praise thee.

The holy Church throughout all the world doth acknowledge thee;

The Father of an infinite Majesty;

Thine honourable, true and only Son;

Also the Holy Ghost, the Comforter.

Thou art the King of Glory, O Christ.

Thou art the everlasting Son of the Father.

When thou tookest upon to deliver man, thou didst not abhor the Virgin's womb.

When thou hadst overcome the sharpness of death,

Thou didst open the Kingdom of Heaven to all believers.

Thou sittest at the right hand of God, in the Glory of the Father.

We believe that thou shalt come to be our Judge.

We therefore pray thee, help thy servants, whom

thou hast redeemed with thy precious blood.

Make them to be numbered with thy Saints in glory everlasting.

O Lord, save thy people, and bless thine heritage.

Govern them, and lift them up for ever.

Day by day we magnify thee;

And we worship thy Name, ever world without end.

Vouchsafe, O Lord, to keep us this day without sin.

O Lord, have mercy upon us,

O Lord, let thy mercy lighten upon us, as our trust is in thee.

O Lord, in thee have I trusted; let me never be confounded.

(Attributed to Niceta of Remisiana, fourth-century bishop of what is now Eastern Serbia)

❦ Nine ❦

*L*ongsuffering Love

Whether or not we appreciate it, suffering is part of our life in Christ. In us, we carry the life of One who suffered—the crucified One, the One who was misunderstood, mistreated, and pursued unto death. He Himself lives in us, and He still suffers, in us and through us, as we convey His longsuffering love to the world. Our faith holds His crude and bloodstained cross as its central symbol. Accepting our suffering is a good part of what He means when He says, "take up your cross and follow me" (Matthew 16:24; Mark 8:34; 10:21).

Often I am asked why I put so much emphasis on such an uncomfortable subject as suffering. I can only reply, "Because it is required." You can't miss all the times suffering is mentioned in the Bible by Jesus and those who followed Him. "For it has been granted to you on behalf of Christ not only to believe on him, but also to suffer for him" (Philippians 1:29, NIV). "For if we be dead with him, we shall also live with him. If we suffer, we shall also reign with him" (2 Timothy 2:11b-12a, KJV).

The suffering of Jesus includes not only physical pain, but also emotional and spiritual agony. From the moment

He was born in a stable and the world for the first time heard the voice of God wailing as a newborn, He suffered. As Jesus' suffering included the full range of human experiences, so does ours. I fall back on a simple definition of suffering: "having what you don't want, or wanting what you don't have." That pretty much covers the matter—everything from the grossest injustices to the quarrel you had this morning with your spouse.

I don't need to tell you that this is an unpopular approach to life. Our society has become obsessed with comfort and fun and personal fulfillment. We are accustomed to fixing things or finding experts to solve every problem. We get impatient when traffic lights malfunction or we are sick for too long. We are not legendary heroes or heroines. We are not gluttons for punishment. We are only ordinary folks who get out of very comfortable beds in the morning, brush our teeth with running water, put on whatever we like to wear, and eat whatever we want for breakfast. Our lives generally don't seem to call for much courage. We are so accustomed to luxury it ruins our day if the air conditioner quits or the waiter says they're fresh out of cherry cheesecake. We expect to get things fixed—fast. When we can't, we are at a loss.

Who can compare sufferings? They are unique as each sufferer is unique. "The heart knows its own bitterness" (Proverbs 14:10, NEB). We respond according to our temperaments. Some cast about for solutions, stew, fret, rage, deny the facts. Some sink into an oblivion of self-recrimination or pity. Some chalk it all up to somebody else's fault. Some pray. But all of us may be tempted to conclude that because we are uncomfortable, God doesn't love us.

Our problems cannot always be fixed, but they can always be accepted as the very will of God for now, and that turns them into something beautiful. Perhaps it is like the field wherein lies the valuable treasure. We must *buy the field*. It is no sun-drenched meadow embroidered with wildflowers. It is a bleak and empty place, but once we know it contains a jewel the whole picture changes. The empty scrap of forgotten land suddenly teems with possibilities. Here is something we can not only accept, but something worth selling everything to buy.

Saved to Suffer

Jesus laid it right on the line when He said, "In this world you will have trouble. But take heart! I have overcome the world" (John 16:33, NIV). Although He healed every imaginable sickness and is still capable of doing so, He didn't promise to fix everything in this world. Instead, He equipped us to persevere through trials and to bear our scars with dauntless faith. And He helps us understand *why* suffering is necessary.

Let's settle it once and for all—suffering happens to everyone and it happens daily. How often do we hear people say, "I just don't understand why God would make So-and-So suffer. She's such a good person." Or, "Why would God ever allow such a terrible thing to happen to such a wonderful family?"

The apostle Peter wrote, "My friends, do not be bewildered by the fiery ordeal that is upon you, as though it were something extraordinary. It gives you a share in Christ's sufferings, and that is cause for joy" (1 Peter 4:12-13, NEB). When we remember that Peter was writing his letter to exiles, we can try to imagine all the various kinds of suffering that were involved for them. They had been banished from their homes, separated from their loved ones, and cut off from their livelihoods, all through no fault of their own. Their children had forgotten the homelands cherished in their parents' memories. Some had died.

Peter understood deeply how they were feeling and he was familiar with the quite natural human tendency to be bewildered when you're in the middle of trouble. He does not deny that it is "fiery." He calls it an ordeal, which it is, but he tells them it's nothing out of the ordinary. It is what any of us ought to expect in one form or another, as long as we're following Jesus. What else should we expect?

Jesus told us we would have to give up the right to ourselves, take up His cross, and follow. He said we would
have to enter the kingdom of God "through much tribula-
tion." We were told we should expect a steep and narrow
road, so why should we be so bewildered to find it steep
and narrow? The thrilling, heart-lifting truth that Peter
speaks of is that in this very ordeal, whatever it is, we are
being granted an unspeakably high privilege: a share in
Christ's sufferings, and that, Peter says, is cause for joy.

Sometimes people wonder how on earth *their* kind of
trouble can possibly have anything to do with Christ's sufferings. Ours are certainly nothing in comparison with
His. We are not being crucified. Our burden is certainly
not the weight of the sins of the world. No, but in all our
afflictions He is afflicted. If we receive them in faith—faith
that they are permitted by a Father who loves us, faith that
He has an eternal purpose in them—we can offer them
back to Him so that He can transform them. If, like Paul,
we want to know Him and the power of His resurrection,
we must also know the fellowship of His sufferings. The
only way to enter that fellowship is to suffer. Can we say,
Yes, Lord—even to that?

Our Suffering Is a Cause for Thanksgiving
Paul tells us that if we endure suffering well, we can therefore exult in the hope of the divine splendor that is to be
ours. "More than this, let us even exult in our present suf-

ferings, because we know that suffering trains us to endure" (Romans 5:3, NEB). No normal person enjoys suffering. To "exult," however, is an action verb. It means to leap for joy, to be jubilant. It is said that when St. Francis of Assisi was persecuted, he literally danced in the street for joy. He was simply being obedient to Jesus' command to rejoice when men revile you and persecute you. You can rejoice only if you take the long view, however—the view that sees the great reward in heaven. You certainly can't rejoice if all you see is the present persecution. "Endurance brings proof that we have stood the test, and this proof is the ground of hope. Such a hope is no mockery, because God's love has flooded our inmost heart through the Holy Spirit he has given us" (Romans 5:4-5, NEB).

What if we aren't able to endure very well? What if all we have is pain and emptiness? What if, like the destitute widow of Zarephath, we have used up our flour and oil, and we are starving and fearful? In response to the prophet Elijah's request, the widow offered him the remnants of her provisions and "there was food for him and her family for a long time" (1 Kings 17:15, NEB). We too can "offer up" our meager scraps, our widowhood, our destitution—even that which we have incurred through our own sinfulness or foolishness. All we can give Him is that which He has given us in the first place. Although our "assigned portion and cup" (Psalm 16:5) seems to be a strange mixture of good and bad, it is all He asks of us. We can look up and rejoice.

Longsuffering Job is always our prime example of one who could convert the worst news into worship. A messenger came to tell him that all of his sons and daughters had just been killed in the collapse of a building.

At this, Job got up and tore his robe and shaved his head. Then he fell to the ground in worship and said:

> *"Naked I came from my mother's womb,*
> *and naked I will depart.*
> *The Lord gave and the Lord has taken away;*
> *may the name of the Lord be praised."*
>
> JOB 1:20-21, NIV

All our pain can be turned into praise.

Our Suffering Is Pruning

I happen to be notorious for my ability to kill any plant my husband brings into the house. He knows what to expect. He says, "Where shall I put it so you can kill it?" But even those of us with brown thumbs can appreciate the fact that vines and many other plants need to be pruned in order to bear a good crop. "I am the true vine, and my Father is the gardener. He cuts off every branch in me that bears no fruit, while every branch that does bear fruit he trims clean so that it will be even more fruitful"

(John 15:1-2, NIV). Besides guaranteeing increased fruitfulness, John 15 gives us other reasons for suffering, such as purification, refinement, sanctification, maturity, and power. Such a harvest makes us fit for the kingdom of God.

Once we visited Spain just after the vineyards had been pruned. The vines were cut back practically to the ground, leaving nothing but little stumps. It was hard to imagine that from those stubby remains would grow healthy vines bearing heavy clusters of juicy grapes. The pruning process makes us look and feel like those vines.

Miss Lilias Trotter, an Englishwoman who was a missionary to Algeria at the turn of the twentieth century, had no impressive results of her missionary labors to exhibit. She had accepted poverty and considered herself to be "buried" with Christ, her grave sealed, as she said, that nothing but the risen life of the Lord Jesus should come forth.

A group of Sunday school leaders (of which my grandfather happened to be one, and my father, nine years old, was allowed to go along) visited her in 1907, asking to "see the work."

"Our first feeling was one of dismay," wrote Miss Trotter.

What could we show them in an hour? And again, what had we to show Americans with their big ideas and keen business minds—no hospitals, no schools, little organization, and no results to speak of for twenty years' fight in Algiers. Then came the clue in the old saying, "Difficulty is the very atmosphere of miracle." We brought the problem to God, and bit by bit, as we prayed, the outline of a programme evolved. We decided to show in all honesty, not what we *had* done, but what had *not* been done, and believe in God to use the very weakness of it all.

The day arrived, and the group long outstayed the time as she showed them the maps she had arranged around her courtyard, "with their woefully thin firing line of stations, and the still sadder record given by tiny red flags of places visited once, and left again to their darkness; and photographs of the pathetic Christless faces of inland tribes."

The outcome? Before the ship carrying the Americans reached Naples, they had raised enough money to support six missionaries for three years. The Algiers Mission Band was constituted and from that time forward, Miss Trotter's arduous work began to bear clusters of grapes.

We Suffer to Have a Share in Christ's Sufferings

We may have been under the impression that the only kinds of sufferings that "count" for Christians are the ones that come because of our testimony for Christ. We can't identify with the experience we read about in Acts 5:41:

"The apostles left the Sanhedrin, rejoicing because they had been counted worthy of suffering disgrace for the Name" (NIV). We recognize that martyrs share in Christ's sufferings. Paul certainly suffered because of his testimony for Christ.

However, *all* of our sufferings were included when Peter wrote, "to the degree that you share the sufferings of Christ, keep on rejoicing" (1 Peter 4:13, NASB) or when Paul wrote, "For to you it has been granted for Christ's sake, not only to believe in Him, but also to suffer for His sake" (Philippians 1:29, NASB). Most of our sufferings for Him are very hidden, not at all public. Our heartbreaks, our disappointments, our hurts may seem relatively trivial. Yet that's where the "rubber meets the road."

In the daily mail, I sometimes get critical letters. Even one expression of disapproval, regardless of how carefully stated or how many positive missives have arrived the same day, affects me, and I can't seem to stop feeling hurt. However, I can respond to such slights in faith. "Lord, you read this letter before I did. You know how this makes me feel. I give it to you." In some small way, saying that makes me able to share in Christ's sufferings.

Colossians 1:24 is perhaps the most definitive, and at the same time the most mysterious of the passages about our sharing Christ's suffering. Paul says, "I am now rejoicing in my sufferings for your sake, and in my flesh I am completing what is lacking in Christ's afflictions for the sake of his body, that is, the church" (NRSV). Granted, none of us will ever attain the stature of the great apostle Paul, yet I believe we can claim some small share in completing what is lacking in the afflictions of Christ.

We are permitted to help fill up some kind of a quota. Whatever sufferings we Christians endure and offer back to Christ somehow help to fill a small percentage of it. Whereas many of the other scriptural reasons for my suffering are for my sake, this one is for the sake of the body of Christ, for the sake of the completion of the preparation of the bride of Christ. We, like our Lord, become broken bread and poured-out wine for the sake of others. It is only while we are alive on this earth that we have a chance to help fill that quota of sufferings. We won't be able to do it any longer when we get to heaven.

We Suffer to Share the Glory

Although I can't claim to understand what it means, I know that one thing I will be able to do when I get to heaven is to "reign with Him"—if I have suffered. Romans 8:17 tells us, "We are God's heirs and all that Christ inherits will belong to all of us as well! Yes, *if we share in his sufferings*, we shall certainly share in his glory" (PHILLIPS). "If we suffer, we shall also reign with him" (2 Timothy 2:11b-12a, KJV).

When he was a young man, Jim Elliot wrote in his diary, "I shall not reign; I have not suffered." It's true that his life was relatively short and pain-free—up until the last few hours of it. From tapes made for me by two of the men who actually did the spearing, I know that Jim's death was not fast and easy. Another eyewitness, a woman who watched from the jungle, gave me a blow-by-blow description and verified that there was great suffering on that river beach. He suffered after all.

There is a mysterious process that goes into operation when we suffer for Christ. "For our light affliction, which is but for a moment, worketh for us a far more exceeding and eternal weight of glory" (2 Corinthians 4:17, KJV). A "weight of glory"? Picture an old-fashioned scales with two pans suspended on an arm. I can put all the troubles I ever had in my whole life into one pan, and the weight of glory in the other pan will still outweigh it. Those troubles will go up in the balance like feathers. This is quite mysterious, but we can believe that it's true.

We Suffer to Show the Life of Jesus

Paul writes, "Every day we experience something of the death of Jesus, so that we may also show the power of the life of Jesus in these bodies of ours. Yes, we who are living are always being exposed to death for Jesus' sake, so that the life of Jesus may be plainly seen in our mortal lives" (2 Corinthians 4:10-11, PHILLIPS).

This passage became very real to me when I was living with the Aucas in a little wall-less house. I couldn't speak to these people and they had no idea why I was there. My physical surroundings were, to say the least, something less than comfortable. I had to die all kinds of little deaths. I had absolutely no privacy; everybody knew everything that was going on. Two boys next door watched everything I did and commented on it, accompanied with sound effects, announcing it to the general public. I got tired of people coming in and taking down the one little Indian carrying net in which I kept my one change of clothing. The Indians, who wore no clothing at all, marveled that I possessed not only the one skirt and blouse I had on, but an extra set, which they felt I should give them. I lived there and tried to learn their language from scratch and endured the bugs and the bats and the threat of snakes and the food that was rather limited. It would have been easy to give up. But this passage reminded me that I was there to die daily—thousands of little deaths—so that I would be an empty vessel into which the life of Christ could be poured.

The photographer for LIFE magazine who came to Ecuador after Jim was killed was not a Christian. He could not understand why we were there in the first place. "What is a missionary?" he asked us.

I said to him, "I know the answer that I am going to give you is a true one, but it is not going to make any sense to you." He'd had missionaries coming at him from all sides, shoving tracts and books at him, and the life of Christ was not in those efforts.

He said, "Those people with their tracts will never make me a Christian, but you might make me a Christian with the diaries of Jim Elliot." Through the privations and death of a dedicated Christ-bearer, he saw the life of Jesus.

Thou Hast Enlarged Me

With Paul we can "boast all the more gladly" about our weaknesses, "so that Christ's power may rest on [us]." We delight "in weaknesses, in insults, in hardships, in persecutions, in difficulties," having learned that we are strongest when we are weakest (2 Corinthians 12:8b-10, NIV). "Not only so, but we also rejoice in our sufferings, because we know that suffering produces perseverance; perseverance, character; and character, hope. And hope does not disappoint us, because God has poured out his love into our hearts by the Holy Spirit, whom he has given us" (Romans 5:3-5, NIV).

There is a marvelous line in the first verse of Psalm 4: "Thou hast enlarged me when I was in distress." The psalmist is not rejoicing that God has set him free from his suffering. Instead, he is appreciating the fact that his distress has "enlarged" him, as it did for Joseph in Pharaoh's prison, where "iron entered into his soul" (Psalm 105:18).

We suffer. We share in Christ's sufferings. We are purified. And our souls are enlarged.

Ten

The Hope of Glory

Throughout these ten chapters, I have been examining a foundational concept, namely that we can't begin to live the life of a Christ-bearer on our own, and that the sum of the matter is that *in us* we have Christ, and He makes it possible for us to show the world what the kingdom of God is like, "the mystery that has been kept for ages and generations but is now disclosed to the saints. To them God has chosen to make known among the Gentiles the glorious riches of this mystery, which is Christ in you, the hope of glory" (Colossians 1:26, NIV).

Christ *in you*. Christ *in me*. When we surrender our lives to Him, He comes into our spirits. And "he who is joined to the Lord is one spirit with him" (1 Corinthians 6:17, NKJV). Therefore, it is not two spirits, mine and His, holding hands as it were, or locked together in the same room. It's two spirits melding into one. The Creator and Sustainer of the universe dwells in the depths of my being. This does not make me a god, but it makes me more and more like God.

Every one of us can be "filled with all the fullness of God" (Ephesians 3:19). This is fullness in the fullest sense, the fullness of "Him who fills all in all" (Ephesians 1:23). Now "it is no longer I who live, but Christ lives in me" (Galatians 2:20). My old life has been superseded by the fullest Life possible. Christ, the hope of glory is here in me—and He is in you.

This is not to say that we are clones. Our Creator made each of us as different as He did the snowflakes. Enfleshed in humanity, He displays the infinite number of facets of His character. My personality is not all bubbly and fun and charming, but yours might be. Each of us shows forth a set of God's traits. Christ, the hope of glory, dwells in each of us and works in us differently, causing us to reflect His glory to those around us.

We need to revive our awareness of what that hope of glory can do in us and through us. Jesus Christ Himself lives in us and He is our hope of glory. This is something far, far beyond our wildest hopes and dreams. Over the course of our lives as Christians, we will become more like Him because He is working in us, and we will thereby taste heaven, but we will never be able to fully understand the glory of His kingdom until we get there. I wonder if one of the reasons God doesn't give us more clues about what heaven is going to be like is that we would never manage to keep our minds on our work if we knew. It would be like telling little children ahead of time where the Christmas presents are hidden.

God Calls Us By Name

What He does tell us is that He calls us by name, personally, daily. "Thus saith the Lord that created thee,... I have called thee by thy name; thou art mine" (Isaiah 43:1, KJV). People who engage in public relations know the importance of using a person's name. Whether or not we call people by a name and what name we use are deeply significant, often a dead giveaway of our attitude toward a person. (For example, contrast the husband who calls his wife "sweetheart," with the one who routinely calls her "mommy.")

In an airport, most of us pay little attention to the announcements coming over the public address system, precisely because it is the general public that is being addressed. But if we hear our own name, we come to life very quickly. When Mary went to the garden tomb on the first Easter morning, she did not know the Lord right away. She took Him to be the gardener until He spoke her name. That brought recognition. Instantly she responded, "Master!" In recognition of our individuality, the Shepherd of our souls issues a personal call. Sheep know the voice of the shepherd and will not follow a stranger. "He calls his own sheep by name and leads them out" (John 10:3, RSV).

I once took a little dog through a course in obedience

school. One of the lessons he had to learn was to respond to my voice only. There were forty-nine other dogs and their masters in the circle, and commands were given by more than one person at a time. Each dog had to distinguish, out of all the noise, the one voice that called to him. So do we who are trainees in God's obedience school. We learn to love the sound of His voice, and our obedience to Him, in matters large and small, changes us into His image, "from glory to glory" (2 Corinthians 3:18). That is a promise.

We are supposed to be *saints*. Saints are not merely that small number of men and women who have been canonized officially. According to the New Testament, saints are those who belong to Christ, in whom Christ lives. We are meant to be saints not only when we get to heaven, but right here in this world—without necessarily having our circumstances changed. We won't become storybook princesses or heroes, but we will be changed into the image of Christ.

Response Is What Counts

What counts the most is our *response* to everything. It is not what happens to us, but how we respond and how we look to God for strength and guidance. Two thieves were crucified next to Jesus. One of them recognized his guilt, understood who Jesus was and what He could do, and responded with repentance for his sin. Jesus told him, "Today, you will be with me in Paradise." The other responded with venom. Their immediate circumstances were unchanged. Both thieves were still nailed to their crosses, dying. Their response made all the difference.

Once I was in turmoil about some things somebody had said to me. I lay awake at night, mentally enacting whole scenes and conversations in which we would "have it out," dragging everything into consciousness, pitting what she said against what I said, what she did against what I did, defending and offending, complaining and explaining.

Then I read this: "Turn from evil. Let that be the medicine to keep you in health" (Proverbs 3:7-8). And this: "Love is kind. Love is never quick to take offense. Love keeps no score of wrongs. There is nothing love cannot face; there is no limit to its faith, its hope, and its endurance" (1 Corinthians 13:4-5, 7). Then I found the prescription for what ailed me: "Let your bearing toward one another arise out of your life in Christ Jesus.... He made himself nothing ... humbled himself ... accepted death" (Philippians 2:5, 7-8, NEB).

What a relief! I no longer had to cogitate about how to handle my feelings or plot and plan how to confront my friend or rehearse just what I would say. My bearing toward her would arise *out of my life in Christ Jesus.* I couldn't do it myself. He could, and He would enable me.

Trusting Him to do that, I calmed down. With an untroubled spirit, I could love her, still at a distance, but without the inner turmoil. He helped me from start (bringing my attention to His Word) to finish (drawing peace and love from His holy wells of supply)—and I became a little more like my Master.

How Does This Transformation Happen?

Day after day, Christ is formed in me in the midst of the circumstances of my life, because those circumstances are the visible evidence of the will of God. An all-loving and all-wise Father apportions everything to me, measuring it out with care to achieve a holy makeover. Does Elisabeth need more patience? More love? More trust? More joy? Does she need help in her response to Me?

To love God is to love His will. As I learn to love His will, I am united with Christ, who loved His Father and the Father's will to the radical degree that He allowed Himself to be crucified. As I love God and His will and allow myself to be crucified with Him, my hope of glory becomes brighter and brighter. Increasingly, I am opening myself to the pervading presence of His Spirit in me.

The apostle Paul wrote, "I have been crucified with Christ and I no longer live, but Christ lives in me. The life I live in the body, I live by faith in the Son of God, who loved me and gave himself for me. I do not set aside the grace of God, for if righteousness could be gained through the law, Christ died for nothing!" (Galatians 2:20-21, NIV). Paul is almost stumbling with excitement over his words, pouring them out, trying to articulate in human terms this mind-boggling mystery. He goes back and forth: "have been *crucified*" ... "*I live.*" Somehow, this paradoxical, inexplicable transformation takes place.

Unruly Wills

The Book of Common Prayer contains Collects, which are short prayers comprising ideas gathered or collected from the day's readings. Here's the one for the Fifth Sunday in Lent:

> Almighty God, you alone can bring into order the unruly wills and affections of sinners. Grant your people grace to love what you command and desire what you promise, that among the swift and varied changes of the world our hearts may surely there be fixed, where true joys are to be found, through Jesus Christ our Lord, who lives and reigns with you and the Holy Spirit, one God, now and forever. *Amen.*

It takes no specially profound understanding of the Bible to know that we do not begin to measure up to its standards. And nothing is more difficult to conform to them than our "unruly wills and affections." On our own strength, we are not going to get beyond our natural emotions. But God wants to transform (Yes, He really does!) every aspect of our inward selves as we bring our wills and feelings under the control of His lordship. The glorious character of Jesus Christ is formed in me as I bring my will and affections to Him—every one of my emotions, all my decisions, every ounce of my willpower, voluntarily putting myself under His loving tutelage and authority.

The Difference Christ Makes

Someone who faithfully follows Jesus can expect, inevitably, to be transformed into someone who radiates peace in the midst of turmoil and bustle, a person of meekness and quietness of spirit even when under provocation.

Meekness and quietness of spirit is not the same as weakness. Moses is said to have been the meekest man who ever lived, yet he had great strength. We are being changed into the likeness of Jesus, who was both the *Lamb* of God and the *Lion* of Judah.

Not much in our world teaches us to be meek. My college debate training certainly didn't teach me about meekness and submissiveness. I am not naturally submissive anyway. My mother used to tell me, "Don't argue with me, Bets. Do what I say." Even when she was very old and we had friendly arguments, she'd concede, "Well, I never *could* argue with you!" We had very different personalities. But Jesus Christ has been working in me for all the years I have known Him. He is making a difference in me, making me meek, gentle, humble.

Meekness is one of the fruits of the Spirit and it is a key to the troublesome matter of judgmentalness. If we are truly meek (caring not at all for self-image or reputation) we will speak the truth as we see it. Contrary to the notion that the only pronouncement in the Bible about judgment is "judge not," we have been *commanded* to judge ourselves and our fellow Christians. (If you find that hard to believe, see 1 Corinthians 5 and Galatians 6:1.) But we must judge in love, recognizing our own sinful capabilities and never-ending need for grace, as well as the limitations of our understanding. If we are to do the will of God in this matter, we must do it by faith as we do every other thing, taking the risk of being at times mistaken. We may misjudge, but at least we can be honest and charitable. If we were not to judge at all we would have to erase from our Christian vocabulary the word *is*, for whatever follows that word is a judgment: Mama is a cook, Davey is a baseball player, George is unemployed. Many of those judgments are positive ones.

Jesus told us to love our enemies. How are we to know who they are without judging? He spoke of "dogs," "swine," "hypocrites," "liars," as well as of friends, followers, rich men, the great and the small, the humble and the proud, "he who hears you and he who rejects you," old and new wineskins, the things of the world and the things of the kingdom. Jesus, the Meek One with whom we are yoked, the One who cared least of all for His own welfare, made those judgments.

One of the outstanding characteristics of a meek spirit is teachability. Jesus said, "Come to me, all you who are weary and burdened, and I will give you rest. Take my yoke upon you and learn from me, for I am gentle and humble in heart, and you will find rest for your souls. For my yoke is easy and my burden is light" (Matthew 11:29, NIV). To take His yoke upon ourselves and learn from Him means we bend our necks under the same yoke that Jesus did when He submitted to the will of the Father. The picture is of the double-oxen yoke, two oxen walking side by side at the same speed, working in harmony. Jesus calls it *my* yoke, which means He has allowed it to be laid upon His neck first. He's not asking us to bend our necks to anything with which He hasn't been saddled already. With His yoke firmly across our spirits, we find it easier to "walk the walk." Getting in step with Him is almost unavoidable. We are a team.

The Glory of Peace

Jesus has a kind of peace that the world can never give, and He promises to share it with us.

I know people who literally bring peace into a room. One of them is my dear friend, Myra Walters, who is a Welsh lady and a medical doctor, one of the sweetest, quietest, calmest people I have ever known. During the last weeks of my husband Add's life, she would come to the house every day for ten or fifteen minutes just to see him. We three knew that there wasn't anything she could do for him as a doctor, but she would just walk into his room like an angel of the Lord, bringing peace. I could see my husband relax as every day she would walk over to the bed, take his hand, bend way down, and say, "Tell me how you feel, Add." It was as if he was carried through from one day to the next by God's peace, brought in by Myra.

My father gave me Isaiah 41:10 when I went away to boarding school: "Fear thou not; for I am with thee: be not dismayed; for I am thy God: I will strengthen thee; yea, I will help thee; yea, I will uphold thee with the right hand of my righteousness." God will keep that promise for all of us. Christ is in me, He who is the hope of glory.

Whenever we feel we are falling far short, let's remember another wonderful promise from Isaiah 50:7, "For the Lord God will help me; therefore shall I not be confounded: therefore have I set my face like a flint, and I know that I shall not be ashamed." If you feel you have made such a mess of things that you will never reflect the image of Christ, remember *you* are not responsible to do it. The life of Christ *in* you will reproduce itself.

When we are redeemed, we become new creatures. Anything becomes possible. Jesus is in the business of making us new men and women. He died so that He could live His life in us, making us Life-givers.

> *When you call, the Lord will answer. "Yes, I am here," he will quickly reply.... The Lord will guide you continually, watering your life when you are dry and keeping you healthy, too. You will be like a well-watered garden, like an everflowing spring.*
>
> ISAIAH 58:9-11, NLT

For a complete list of other books and resources
from Elisabeth Elliot, visit her website at
www.elisabethelliot.org